Mastering
BUSINESS
Presentations

NATIONAL INSTITUTE OF BUSINESS MANAGEMENT

SPECIAL REPORT BMBP

AUTHOR
Morey Stettner

EDITOR
Kathy A. Shipp

EDITORIAL DIRECTOR
Joe McGavin

PUBLISHER
Phillip Ash

ISBN 1-880024-53-5

"This publication is designed to provide accurate and authoritative information in regard to the subject matter covered. It is sold with the understanding that the publisher is not engaged in rendering legal, accounting or other professional service. If legal advice or other expert assistance is required, the services of a competent professional person should be sought."
—*From a Declaration of Principles jointly adopted by a committee of the American Bar Association and a committee of publishers and associations.*

Contents

Introduction

A Presenter's Best Friend

"If you don't care about giving a speech, get psyched to do it. That'll make you nervous—and that's good! If you're not nervous, you'll be flat."

—C. Richard Reese
CEO, Iron Mountain Inc.

If you could read presenters' minds 24 hours before they're scheduled to deliver a speech, you could largely determine whether they are going to succeed or fail.

✔ **Top speakers** think like winners. They review their outline enthusiastically and conclude they've crafted a tight, well-organized talk. They tell themselves the purpose of their speech is to quench their listeners' thirst for information and insight. They visualize receiving a rousing ovation from an appreciative audience.

✔ **Terrified speakers** fight off dread. As the clock ticks down to the Big Event, fear immobilizes them. They assume they're going to embarrass themselves, whether by opening with a joke that bombs, losing their place, sweating, misstating a point or putting the audience to sleep. They visualize people walking out early, shaking their heads in disgust or heckling them.

Even though public speaking may not qualify as one of your top 10 favorite activities, remember this: If you dwell on how much you hate it and how bad you are at it, you'll make matters worse. Every time you tell someone, "I just can't give speeches," you reinforce a self-perceived weakness. You become entrenched in a dangerously narrow comfort zone where you'll miss opportunities to persuade others and express your opinions. Worst of all, by setting such low expectations, you'll sabotage yourself and deliver a flat, boring presentation that befits your dismal self-image.

To overcome your self-imposed terror, you're going to need practice. That means accepting every chance that comes along to build your confidence by speaking up. For example, you should:

• Volunteer to serve as spokesperson when you're in a breakout group at a seminar.

• Raise your hand and stand to ask a question when you're in a large audience.

• Offer to step in and lead a staff meeting when your boss gets called away suddenly.

- Take every opportunity to give a toast, serve on a panel or introduce a guest speaker.

Don't believe speech coaches who promise "you'll never be nervous again." That's a pipe dream. Instead, you want to embrace your fear and channel it to best advantage. In this book we'll show you how.

Jitters on the Loose

Fear of public speaking runs rampant in Western culture. Surveys often show that Americans dread it more than death, snakes, airline travel and countless other phobias.

Most speakers respond to the jitters by freezing up. From the moment they learn they're going to give a presentation, trepidation sets in. They gulp hard, dream up worst-case scenarios and start plotting ways to back out. The week before a speech can turn into a living hell of sleepless nights and frayed nerves.

Ironically, the best approach to handling the pre-speech jitters is to *welcome* them. By thinking, "I'm nervous. Good. That will give me the energy to succeed," you can reframe your anxiety as a positive force. Remember this age-old advice for public speakers: *"Everyone has butterflies. The key is to get them to fly in formation."*

It's natural to feel nervous before a speech. In fact, it's often a prerequisite to doing a good job. It's the way you *respond* to the jitters that determines the odds of succeeding. If you deaden your senses and speak like a zombie, you'll lose any chance of connecting with your audience. But by reminding yourself that your jitters are normal and inevitable, you'll approach the stage as a warmer, fully dimensional person who's striking up a conversation from the front of the room.

Beware of these destructive responses to having a case of the jitters:

■ *I'll fake it.* If you're frightened of public speaking, you may resort to a personality makeover. For example, many speakers who aren't especially funny in their everyday lives figure they must open with a slam-dunk joke to establish their comic credentials and win over the audience. But the joke they wind up telling backfires because they're not good at the delivery. Had they simply opened with a startling statistic or a succinct story—perhaps interwoven with a sincere expression of good will—they would have enthralled the audience from the outset.

■ *I'm helpless.* You fret over things you can't control: The time of day is all wrong for your speech, the room has bad acoustics, the speaker before you will turn the group against you, and so on. The more you concentrate on circumstances beyond your control, the faster your jitters will multiply.

■ *I just want to survive.* You tell yourself, "If I don't screw it up, I'll be fine." That's setting a low bar! Likening a speech to fighting a war will suffocate your personality and strip away the sparkle and genuineness you'll need to earn the audience's respect. You'll be so busy rushing to finish and viewing your listeners as a barrier to overcome that you'll neglect to establish a bond with them.

Bottom line: Manage your jitters by reminding yourself of what the audience wants: to learn something. They're not sitting in cruel judgment, waiting to attack you. They don't want to be bored or fed platitudes. They hate wasting their time as much as you dread giving a speech. These reminders won't wipe away your nervousness, but they should help funnel your fear into communicating in a lively, trustworthy manner.

Fear's Ripple Effect

An old television commercial for deodorant advised, "Never let 'em see you sweat." That also applies to public speaking.

If you're scared as you walk to the podium, that's your business. The audience doesn't need to know. In fact, it's better that they *not* know. The minute you let fear overtake you, you're doomed. Your voice will lose its resonance, and you may lapse into a monotone. The pitch of your voice will probably rise too—making it virtually impossible to capture and keep the audience's attention.

Your body won't cooperate either. As if succumbing to the weight of fear, your shoulders will droop. You'll slouch and fidget. Instead of taking a few steps occasionally to build drama and signal a transition to a new point in your speech, you'll pace wildly like a caged tiger. You may blink your eyes uncontrollably or unconsciously scratch your head.

Exercise 1: Mind Your Attitude

Use this assessment tool to help you pinpoint potential trouble spots. Check any of the statements below that describe your feelings about public speaking:

_____ I'm fine when I prepare my thoughts, but when I must speak off the cuff, I panic.

_____ I'm OK addressing strangers, but I hate standing up and talking to people I know.

_____ I'm fine if I can remain seated and talk, but if I have to stand, I feel self-conscious.

_____ I enjoy teaching or explaining things, but I'm uncomfortable giving an opinion or taking sides.

_____ I prefer to give the audience handouts that convey most of the information so that I don't have to add much.

_____ I hit my stride in the middle of my speeches, but I'm never sure how to open and close them.

_____ I give speeches only reluctantly. I never like it.

If you checked any of these statements, you'll need to adopt a more open, receptive attitude so as to conquer even the most adverse situations. By developing strategies to succeed even when your prerequisites for comfort aren't met, you can become a more confident, commanding and flexible speaker.

At the first sign of sweaty or shaking palms, you might overcompensate by wringing your hands constantly. That in turn can become a far more jarring distraction to your audience than if you simply leave your hands alone and gesture naturally.

Finally, fear will mess with your mind. You'll see someone in the audience yawn, and you'll think, "I'm putting everyone to sleep." Your eyes will dart to someone who's frowning, and you'll decide, "They hate me. They really hate me!" In short, you'll assume that one person's behavior represents how the entire audience feels—and your confidence will dissolve rapidly.

You can escape from a fear-induced downward spiral by redirecting your anxiety. Rather than let it suffocate your energy, release it in the form of animated facial expressions, vivid gestures and strategic use of the stage. For example, walking in front of the lectern can show listeners that you're a brave speaker who's determined to connect with them. Depending on the layout of the room, you may want to wander through the aisles or encircle the group to keep everyone's attention. No matter how much fear you're feeling, stepping closer to the audience will boost your confidence and make you look like a bold, gutsy speaker.

Climb the Success Ladder

The goal of this book is to give you practical tools to deliver successful presentations. We begin with chapters on how to organize your ideas, package them effectively and make every minute of rehearsal pay off. We'll identify some potentially debilitating fears and how to overcome them, along with strategies to ace all kinds of presentations—from briefing senior management and leading staff meetings to delivering formal speeches to large audiences.

Mastering the ability to speak dynamically in a range of settings will open career doors. It's a great way to get senior executives to notice you and respect your poise and intelligence. It also helps you command respect from your peers and staff. Best of all, learning to present your ideas forcefully in front of others ensures that you'll earn the credit you deserve. Present your ideas with conviction, and you become a "player," a member of an exclusive club of articulate, confident leaders who tend to rise to the top.

1.

Pick the Right Road Map

"Here are four words to leave out of a speech: 'Unaccustomed as I am ...' The idea is to keep the audience from figuring that out."

—ED MCMAHON
Entertainer

Teresa Lever-Pollary could sense it: Her presentations were becoming lifeless. Even when she discussed the corporate values she held dear as CEO of Utah-based Nightime Pediatrics Clinics Inc., Lever-Pollary knew her message wasn't resonating with either internal or external audiences.

She decided to lace her talks with anecdotes. To find some, she began asking her employees and clients to share their experiences with the company. For example, a nurse told her how one of Nightime's doctors lured an ant from inside a child's ear with a dollop of cake frosting as bait. Then the doctor set the ant free outside, providing a satisfying ending to a story that nicely captured the company's commitment to kind, gentle care.

Lever-Pollary's ability to amass rich stories about Nightime made it much easier for her to communicate the company's mission, according to *Entrepreneur* magazine (February 2001). Eventually, she collected more than 80 anecdotes that made her company come alive.

Regardless of your topic, the first step in delivering a memorable speech is intensive preparation. You must identify your goal, organize your thoughts and, like Lever-Pollary, prepare stories that make it easier to get across your points.

Identify Your Goal

As soon as you know you're going to give a speech, the first question you must ask yourself is "Why am I going to speak?" Explore your purpose. Weigh what you would gain by speaking—and what you would lose by passing up the chance.

You may find it easier to define the goal of your presentation by "talking it out" with a friend or a colleague. Or, if you prefer to prepare on your own, it might help to take notes or tape-record yourself speaking aloud as you cover all your reasons for giving the speech.

Once you're satisfied that you've identified why you're speaking, narrow your focus. Ask yourself, "What do I want my audience to do as a result?" Think in terms of actions you want them to take, beliefs you want them to accept or ideas you want them to consider.

Now comes the hard part. Reduce your goal to one sentence that describes exactly what you want others to do after hearing your presentation. For example:

* *I want my sales force to retain more customers by building ongoing, service-oriented relationships.*

* *I want my employees to cut their error rate in half by applying new tools to improve accuracy.*

* *I want to inspire the audience to donate an average of $10 per person to my favorite cause.*

Notice how the goal begins with "I want" and then targets the audience. That will help you pinpoint what you want listeners to do. The best goals also share these features:

■ **A positive tone.** In one of the examples above, the goal isn't just to have employees stop making mistakes; it's "to cut their error rate in half by applying new tools to improve accuracy." By crafting a positive goal, you add to its appeal. As a rule, compose goals that help you and the audience *move toward* something desirable rather than *move away* from something negative.

■ **A lively verb.** The action word that characterizes your goal will influence how you speak. Replace flat, deadening verbs, such as *be, get* and *have,* with more evocative ones, such as *pounce, entice* and *energize.*

■ **A measurable outcome.** You want a goal that holds you accountable. Don't weaken your speech by deciding you merely want to "raise morale" or "explain a new procedure." Instead, determine how you can measure your progress in a quantifiable way. Set about to "raise morale so employees increase production 10 percent" or "explain a new procedure so that it's ready for implementation by May 1."

Organize Your Thoughts

You may figure that scribbling on a napkin an outline of the main points you want to make will suffice. It won't. Smart speakers know they need a road map to help them reach their destination. They thus create a tidy, sensible organizational structure to support their goal so that they—and the audience—can follow along with ease.

The best way to organize your ideas is to cluster them in threes. Even the most complex speeches can fit into neat structures such as these:

* Problem/cause/solution
* Past/present/future
* Risks/rewards/action plan
* Pros/cons/outcome
* Short-term opportunities/long-term opportunities/pitfalls

By lining up your ideas in a clean, logical manner, you can recover quickly if you lose your place or get distracted during your presentation. Rather than panic, you'll be able to regain momentum by recalling the three-part road map you've created to organize your talk. That will help you return to the point you were making.

Easier to digest

Why three parts? The mind readily grasps ideas bundled in threes, so it's easier for listeners to digest your speech. If you try to divide your presentation into four or more main chapters, it will test the audience's patience or simply overwhelm them. And if you divide your talk into two main sections (i.e., strengths and weaknesses), it will lack the persuasive punch that a third section can provide.

If you're knowledgeable about your topic, you may find it nearly impossible to limit your speech to just three parts. Say you're armed with dozens of reasons why the audience should accept your proposal. You want to cover them all to sway even the most resistant listeners. In truth, however, your refusal to streamline your talk winds up alienating your audience, who will resent being pelted with so much information. *Your* mind may be overflowing with ideas, but your listeners don't need to hear them all.

In fact, you must customize your three-part speech to fit the knowledge level and expectations of the audience. Consider the *fudge principle:* Fishermen don't bait the hook with fudge (i.e., what *they* like to eat); they use worms to appeal to the trout. Similarly, you don't want to overload a speech with your favorite statistics or strongest opinions; rather, you must bait the hook with information that your listeners will eagerly grab.

In deciding how to organize your presentation in threes, empathize with your listeners. Assess their interests, objectives, fears, biases and concerns. Gauge their mood based on the temperature in the room where you'll be speaking, the time of day, what they did in the hour before your speech and even breaking news or sporting events that may preoccupy them.

Your objective is to determine the three most captivating points for your particular audience. For example, when addressing salespeople, discuss the three most exciting profit opportunities you can offer them rather than the technical details about a new sales software program. If you're educating your organization's board of directors about recent budgetary issues, highlight the three most important cost-control measures you've taken. Or, to persuade a group of managers to work as a team, isolate the three most direct, measurable benefits they'll gain by collaborating.

Prepare Stories

In the days after you deliver your speech, chances are the audience won't remember the specifics about the evidence you presented or the proposals you offered. But they will remember a good story.

The best stories begin with an actor, an action and an object that's acted upon. For example:

- *The CEO couldn't stop laughing at the computer screen.*
- *The security guard heard a noise coming from what he thought was an empty conference room.*

- *The plant foreman noticed a snag in the machinery.*

Each of these lines contains the elements of an attention-grabbing story. The actor (CEO, security guard, plant foreman) takes an action (laughs, hears, notices) that involves an object (computer screen, empty room, machinery). Inevitably, your eager listeners will ask themselves, "What happened next?"

The beauty of stories is that they enable you to connect with people. If your audience perceives you as aloof, boring or grandiose, they'll tune out. You need to convince them you're like them. Stories humanize your topic and attract listeners like honey. The first line of an anecdote serves the same purpose as putting your arm around an audience member and saying, "Hey, friend, wait till you hear this!"

Another benefit of a good anecdote: It's easy on the ears. Many business speakers tax their audience with overly complex, stiff or bureaucratic blather. Telling a story, by contrast, enlivens your subject matter and sets you apart from stodgy speakers.

In preparing your stories, keep these pointers in mind:

■ **Identify time, place and activity.** Lace your anecdotes with references to a specific setting. This helps set the scene in vivid terms. Examples:

- *By 8 a.m. I was jammed into the subway train, trying desperately not to sneeze in a stranger's face.*

- *The minute the phone rang, we raced to our desks and prepared to eavesdrop.*

- *The hot sun baked the car, the air conditioning didn't work, and here we were, stuck in rush-hour traffic while a multimillion-dollar deal was occurring just five miles away.*

■ **Speak naturally.** Never write out a story verbatim. You'll strip the life out of the tale, and everyone will know you memorized it. Make sure to include the key elements (clearly introducing an actor, action and object and a time, place and activity), but give yourself the flexibility to improvise a bit.

■ **Keep it moving.** The best anecdotes take less than a minute to tell. Each sentence should advance the story. Poor speakers tend to repeat or restate themselves, rather than build on what they just said to create a smooth narrative flow.

■ **Know your goal.** Choose stories that relate to your theme or provide an entry point for one of the three sections of your speech. Don't just toss in random anecdotes that strike you as "funny" but lack any relevance to the topic.

■ **Tell the truth.** Exaggerate at your own risk. Most listeners can detect an apocryphal story—and they'll dismiss everything else you say if they conclude you're lying. Above all, don't insist, "I swear this is true!" Protest too much and you raise suspicion.

Pick the Best Evidence

At some point, you'll need to dish out some concrete evidence to back up your points. Anecdotes will arouse listeners' interest, but you'll hook them with strong support, ranging from facts to personal experience.

If you're addressing a small, familiar group, think back to how they constructed their arguments. What types of support did they provide? If you're talking to technicians who love spreadsheets and detailed analysis, you'll probably want to line up your data in a tidy, sequential fashion. Or, if you're dealing with senior executives who track broad industry trends or draw conclusions based on visits to company sites, prepare statistics that underlie business trends and share your own findings from your travels in the field.

In structuring your speech, start strong and finish even stronger. As John Quincy Adams said, "The ideas of the audience should be kept in a continually ascending state." Lead up to your conclusion by citing increasingly powerful evidence that builds on what you've already said.

For example, if you plan to give three reasons why the audience should donate to your charity, start by highlighting the efficient use of the funds to fulfill the group's mission. Then discuss why the need is greater this year because of government cutbacks. Wrap up by delivering the clincher: For every dollar in donations, you've enlisted a benefactor who will make a matching gift. You've thus guided the audience down a persuasive path marked by three increasingly powerful arguments in favor of action.

Plan to provide at a minimum one piece of evidence for every major premise of your speech. Forms of common evidence include:

- Facts
- Statistics
- Third-party testimonials
- Your direct observation

■ **Facts** often appeal to business audiences, who like to collect information and draw their own conclusions. Cite facts that listeners can easily remember and pass along to their colleagues and bosses. But don't bog down your speech in a dry recitation of facts that aren't tied to your larger point.

Tip: Cite apparently contradictory facts to draw in the audience. Ask, "How can that be?" Then help everyone understand what's really going on.

■ **Statistics** can help educate an audience that has misconceptions about a topic. The more surprising your stats, the better. Just make sure the audience deems your source as credible.

Use statistics sparingly. Unless you're addressing a roomful of financial types (such as accountants or controllers), throwing too many numbers at your audience will work against you. Most listeners either don't pay much attention to statistics or view numbers with suspicion. If you reel off dozens of studies or show graph after graph to illustrate your point, you risk overloading the audience with information they can't or won't absorb.

■ **Third-party testimonials** allow you to show an association with a respected authority on the topic. In business settings, this works especially well if your "expert" is the CEO or some other influential leader whom everyone respects. Quoting customers can also bolster your argument if your corporate culture emphasizes keeping in touch with them.

■ **Your direct observation** works well if you're speaking to peers who can identify with your experience and probably make similar observations. Getting everyone to nod knowingly at your first-hand evidence bonds you to the audience. Stating what you've seen to support your points usually carries more weight if you're perceived as a credible spokesperson, a veteran in the trenches who has "seen it all."

Maintain a logical sequence

Regardless of the type of evidence you use, present it in a logical sequence. Here are two examples of how to construct a tight, logical flow:

1. **Inductive reasoning** involves beginning with the specific and moving to the general. Thinking inductively forces you to amass enough relevant facts, experiences and data to lead an audience of skeptics to buy into your argument.

   Say you're trying to get your staff to improve its customer service. Rather than starting your speech by insisting on the need for better service, apply the inductive process so that your employees realize for themselves what they must do. Open by lining up facts:

   > *Our customer retention rates dropped 22 percent in one year. I receive an average of eight customer complaints a week, compared to four last year at this time. And when I've called our service line numerous times lately, I've been put on hold for 10 minutes or more each time. It's clear we must take action to improve.*

2. **Deductive reasoning** starts with the end. You organize the presentation with your conclusion first, followed by supporting evidence. A related approach is to open with your conclusion and then analyze the argument and counterargument—or pros and cons—so that your listeners can appreciate opposing views of the issue before ultimately championing your side.

   Trial lawyers, for example, often begin by concluding their client is innocent. Then they'll outline the three best reasons to support their client's innocence, followed by a summary of the opposing lawyer's claims and why they're wrong. By anticipating differing opinions and rebutting them in advance, you can build momentum while robbing adversaries of their chance to sway the audience.

After you've woven evidence into a draft of your speech, review it for balance. Put a check mark in the left margin whenever you include evidence and describe it as a fact, statistic or observation. After marking up your entire draft, you should see checks sprinkled consistently on every page with a mix of several types of evidence. If three or four pages in a row have no check marks, your speech is too general and lacks concrete support.

Open and Close With a Bang

Audiences will remember your introduction and conclusion more than what they heard in between. By arousing their interest from the outset and ending on a note of strength, inspiration and wisdom, you'll satisfy listeners and leave them eagerly wanting more.

At their best, introductions stir excitement. They create rapport between the speaker and audience. Because they seem to enjoy the act of public speaking, great speakers radiate passion and enthusiasm. Rather than sigh and daydream, the audience feels better about sitting there and decides to pay attention.

Even though most speakers figure they must open with a joke, it's actually one of the worst ways to start a speech. Only professional comedians can tell consistently funny jokes that make everyone feel good and draw them into what's to follow. Most of us recite jokes out of obligation, racing through them until we mutter a tepid punch line.

The danger of starting off with a joke? It can backfire. The audience may not laugh, or they may find your humor offensive. In any case, uttering the clichéd line, "Being here today reminds me of a joke . . ." or "Perhaps you've heard the old tale about . . ." sends a clear message that you're a predictable, by-the-book speaker.

Even if you deliver a fresh, tasteful joke, your triumph may prove short-lived. The group may wait for your next spark of wit, only to find that your presentation is no stand-up comedy routine.

Aside from joke-telling, another terrible way to open your speech is to warn the audience that you intend to change their minds. Upon hearing this, they'll hunker down, fold their arms across their chests and think, "Oh, yeah, just make me." It's better to let them discover for themselves the persuasive appeal of your remarks. Alerting them that your goal is to break down their resistance will only cause them to raise their guard even more.

Good openers

So if you skip the opening joke and aren't going to promise to change everyone's mind, how should you begin? Consider these strategies:

■ **Tell a survival story.** Open with an anecdote about someone who's up against seemingly insurmountable odds. Then describe how that individual fought back from the brink to reach some kind of victory. Examples range from adventurers who scale Mount Everest to individuals with terminal diseases who somehow defy medical science and make a complete recovery. End the story by tying it to your topic.

■ **Dangle a challenge or a promise.** Begin by posing a fun challenge to the audience or promising that they'll gain something specific by the end of your speech. For example:

- *I challenge all of you to ask yourself, "Where's the proof?" if I state what appears to be a fact. By the time I'm finished, I want you to tell me if I haven't given you sufficient proof.*

- *I promise that in the next 15 minutes, you'll learn a simple process you can use to calm down almost anyone, especially the most irate hothead!*

- *While I can't guarantee you'll agree with everything I say, I can promise that if we put aside our preconceptions for the next half-hour, we can at the very least forge a new alliance that will benefit us all.*

■ **Pose a mystery.** It's possible to plumb almost any subject for its suspense. For example:

* *A team of brilliant experts fails miserably. Why?*

* *Pulling into your parking space one day at work, you notice something that's out of kilter. What is it?*

* *All the evidence of a recent customer survey points to shoppers' dissatisfaction with a certain product. Yet sales of this product are soaring. Why?*

Audiences love riddles. Introduce your talk by giving them contradictory information to trigger their curiosity. Then move on.

Don't resolve the mystery too soon; keep building suspense throughout your speech, with listeners guessing what you're going to say next. Engage them intellectually, and they'll enjoy and retain more of what you say. Keep them craving more information.

■ **Play a role.** Adopt a fresh point of view, such as addressing your topic from the perspective of a teenager, an alien or an amnesiac. This may sound silly, but it's actually an entertaining way to broaden the audience's outlook and provide a fun twist.

■ **Give a little history.** Situate your subject historically. Put it in context by describing what you'd be saying 10 or 100 years ago about the same topic. Or cite old articles from newspapers or magazines that covered the subject. For example:

* *The other day, I ran across a 1914 newspaper ad. An automaker was advising people to buy his gas-stingy car because the world's petroleum would be used up by 1928.*

Even if you choose a great attention-grabber to open your presentation, there's no guarantee people will remain interested for the duration. You need to capitalize on your captivating kickoff to keep listeners alert.

The best way to do that is to pause for a few seconds after your introduction. Then give a one-sentence overview of what comes next. This assures your audience that you've thought out what you're about to say and you're sure they'll find it compelling. It also signals to everyone that you're moving from the introduction to the body of your remarks.

A superb example comes from Franklin D. Roosevelt's first fireside chat in 1933. He began:

> *I want to talk for a few minutes with people of the United States about banking—with the comparatively few who understand the mechanics of banking but more particularly with the overwhelming majority who use banks for the making of deposits and the drawing of checks.*
>
> *I want to tell you what has been done in the last few days, why it was done, and what the next steps are going to be.*

In less than 30 seconds, Roosevelt defined his audience in his introduction and then set up a road map of what was to follow. In the aftermath of his relaxed, reassuring speech, the public's confidence in the financial system returned after months of panic—and money flowed back into American banks.

Here are some generic examples:

- *We'll look at the social, economic and political repercussions of this issue.*

- *Let's examine with a critical eye the three most compelling features of this proposal.*

- *To better understand this controversial topic, I'll present the pros and cons and then do my best to render a fair verdict.*

A rousing close

To conclude your speech, move beyond a dry summary of what you've already said. End on a rousing call to action, a future-looking rallying cry that envelops the room in positive, hopeful emotions. For example:

- *You've invested 15 minutes in hearing me out. Make your investment pay off by joining me in fighting this battle!*

- *Now you have the tools to get started. Pick at least three tools that make the most sense to you. Apply them this week. Measure the results. Week by week, incorporate these tools into your work routine until you master them. Within three months, you'll reap all kinds of benefits. Let me hear from you when that happens!*

- *All of us have shown our mettle in getting this far. What we've covered today will help us make the best of our organizational upheaval. Now, more than ever, we must dip into our reserves of strength and resilience to persevere—and ultimately prosper.*

At its best, a conclusion builds to a crescendo. The audience can tell by your slower pacing and dramatic delivery that you're about to finish. As you utter your final sentence, they should be poised to applaud appreciatively.

If you're unsure how to end on a high note, remember the three G's: *generous, gracious, grateful.* Conclude by spreading credit around (generous), expressing appreciation for your listeners' attentiveness (gracious) and thanking individuals by name who've assisted you (grateful).

"If you're giving a speech to your CEO or other senior executives, close by thanking everyone on your team for all their hard work," says Ronna Lichtenberg, chief executive of Clear Peak Communications, a New York-based marketing consulting firm. "That implies that you were there, too, burning the midnight oil."

Finally, if you're a guest speaker at a conference or convention, provide a way for listeners to follow up with you. Make sure everyone leaves with your contact information, including your Web site and e-mail address. Here's how:

■ **On the last slide you show, list your phone number, address and e-mail.** Keep the slide visible after you wrap up your speech so that listeners can write down the information after they finish their applause.

■ **Distribute door prizes.** Position aides by the exit doors to hand out your business cards, fliers and giveaway items (pens, pads, calendars) that include your contact information.

■ **If you integrate handouts** into your presentation (such as quizzes or exercises for the group to do during your speech), call everyone's attention to the last page, which should contain your contact information.

Your conclusion should serve as the emotional climax of your speech. Don't squander it by reciting your phone number or e-mail address or writing them on a flip chart. Listeners will inevitably ask you to repeat yourself, yell out that they can't read what's on the chart or simply take down incorrect information. Spare yourself from this by preparing handouts, giveaways and slides that convey this information. That way, you can concentrate on ending on an emotional high.

2.
Research, Write the Right Way

> *"As a general rule, devote about
> 30 minutes of development and prep time
> for every minute of delivery."*
>
> —Tom Mucciolo
> President, MediaNet Inc., a speech coaching firm

Fear of public speaking flows largely from the potential for humiliation. You figure that you might be exposed as an incompetent, as someone who doesn't know all that you should. Combat this anxiety by researching your topic thoroughly.

Once you're convinced you know more than anyone else in the room, your fear will dissipate. You'll gain confidence by realizing that you've gathered far more information than you'll ever need about the subject, and you've handpicked the "best of the best" material to include in your speech.

Veteran speakers don't just research their presentations intensively. They also observe other speakers and become students of effective oratory. When they're stuck listening to a terrible speaker, they resist the urge to fidget or browse the newspaper; instead, they analyze what they don't like about the individual's performance.

Learn in the Audience

Whenever you're seated in the audience, treat it as a learning experience. Take notes not only on the content of the speech but also on the speaker's style. Address questions such as these:

- *How does the speaker integrate fact and opinion into the speech? To what extent is it effective?*

- *Does the speaker's voice—volume, pitch, inflection, tone and tempo—accentuate the speech or detract from it? Why?*

- *Does the speaker seem believable? Why or why not?*

- *How would you rate the speaker's body language? What do you like or not like in terms of hand movements, facial expressions, pacing the stage and posture?*

- *Does the speech seem too short, too long or just right?*

- *Is the speaker dressed appropriately? Are there any visual distractions, such as a loud tie, jangling earrings or poorly pressed clothes?*

The lessons you extract at other speakers' expense can heighten your command when it's your turn to take the stage. Borrow from their strengths and rise above their weaknesses. If the host distributes evaluations after the speech, follow up later and ask for a copy of the results.

Seasoned speakers never stop learning how to improve their presentations. They know it's relatively easy to identify their goal and empathize with a particular audience, but the hard part comes when gathering facts and organizing them in a persuasive, digestible manner. They're always looking for better ways to hook their listeners and keep them attentive from beginning to end.

This chapter explains how to develop an efficient research strategy and compose a solid first draft. By perfecting these two key elements of preparation, you can make the most of your rehearsals later. Every round of practice will improve your command of the topic as you find increasingly powerful ways to bring your subject to life.

Uncover Information Gems

Thanks to the Internet, researching virtually any topic is a breeze. Type some keywords into a search engine, and you're off and running. Within minutes, you'll collect more information than you could possibly need. Sifting for the gems becomes the main challenge.

Some Web sites can help you convey information in a visually appealing manner. For example, if you want to weave historical events into your speech, see *www.ourtimelines.com*. Developed for people interested in researching family history, this site doubles as an excellent resource if you want to personalize a timeline that gives your speech a historical perspective.

Yet you shouldn't rely solely on the Web. Keep files that contain newspaper, magazine or newsletter clippings of startling facts, witty aphorisms or dramatic news accounts. You never know when you'll want to weave such information into a speech. For example, in the book *Lincoln on Leadership*, author Donald T. Phillips writes that "everyone present heard the entire Gettysburg Address, and there were at least 15,000 people in attendance." That's a great fact to slip into your speech if your microphone suddenly malfunctions and you want to recover with a clever ad-lib.

When digging for information to use in an upcoming speech, make sure it passes the CAR test. To make the cut, the information must be *compelling, appropriate* for the audience and come from a *reputable* source.

■ **Compelling.** Research becomes exciting when you come across ironic, fascinating or hard-to-believe information. It should jump out from the page and provoke an instant reaction. If it makes you ask, "So what?" or think, "That's not surprising," it's hardly going to arouse the audience's interest.

The most compelling facts and figures subvert listeners' expectations and make them want to learn more. You want them to think, "Wow! I never would've guessed" or "That doesn't jibe with my belief that . . ." Fill your speech with this kind of great content, and you'll see a handsome payoff from your research.

■ **Appropriate for your audience.** As you collect information, consider how your listeners will respond to it. If you're speaking at a festive occasion such as saluting college graduates, citing statistics about unemployment will backfire. Similarly, quoting the results of a study on sexual dysfunction in a speech about privacy concerns may be stretching it.

Seek out great facts or visual aids that speak for themselves. Just make sure you don't offend anyone. When Stephen Chao, a rising star at the Fox television network, gave a presentation on censorship to a group of VIPs (including then-Secretary of Defense Dick Cheney), he hired a male model to stand by the podium and strip during his speech. Big mistake. Rupert Murdoch, Fox's chairman, watched with disgust and fired Chao soon afterward.

■ **Reputable.** You must evaluate whether a source of information is reliable before deciding to use it. Spreading unsubstantiated rumors or quoting from an obviously biased report may backfire if someone asks you in the Q&A, "What was the source of that study you talked about?" You should feel comfortable divulging this information, not ashamed or unsure.

If you mention survey results or statistics, don't give full source information in your speech. Lacing your presentation with citations—the "talking footnote" approach—will break your rhythm.

Even if your research guides you to information that passes the CAR test, don't feel obliged to use it all. Only include material that advances you toward your goal. Interesting but irrelevant data might confuse listeners and derail your progress.

Look for relevant information wherever you can find it. Enlist friends to clip magazine and newspaper articles related to your topic. Join online chat rooms. Take an informal survey of your colleagues, and report the results in your presentation.

Great material can emerge from unexpected places. An executive at an advertising agency recalls that when he was preparing a big presentation to senior man-

Avoid 'Paralysis of Analysis'

Just as not enough research can undermine your speech, too much can weigh it down. Resist the urge to continue your hunt for information long past the point of diminishing returns.

Some nervous speakers get hooked on rooting out every last fact and figure. They refuse to stop researching and start writing and practicing because they gain comfort (and an illusory sense of control) by collecting mountains of data.

Gathering excessive information in the days just before your presentation may indicate that you don't want to go through with it. A psychologist might interpret your behavior as setting yourself up for failure; after all, if you spend too much time researching at the expense of organizing, writing and rehearsing, you're on track for a disastrous performance.

agement, he took a break to order from a Chinese restaurant. The fortune cookie's message, "The more you say, the less people will remember," became the first sentence of his speech.

Write for the Ear

"You cannot bore people into buying." So said advertising genius David Ogilvy, who understood that the biggest enemy of effective communication is apathy. If people don't care about what you're saying, they'll tune out.

Whether you intend to inform or persuade, you need to construct your speech so that it's easy to listen to. Audiences are more apt to heed your message if you write it in an entertaining way. Some pointers:

■ **Grant control to the listener.** Rather than tell people what to think, give them choices. If you want them to support a certain plan of action, don't say, "Here's what I think is the best way." List three alternatives, with the pros and cons of each. Then let them decide for themselves which option's best, and drop hints along the way.

■ **Arouse fear.** Appeal to the most severe, stinging loss the audience fears the most. Use a phrase such as, "There's one huge mistake that could destroy everything we've gained" or "Left alone, this problem will grow so fast that in one year you'll make sacrifices that you'd never consider today."

■ **Describe nirvana.** Use words to conjure up images so pleasing that your audience cannot help but listen. Tantalize them by saying, "Imagine adding an hour to every day," or asking, "Remember the last time you experienced total inner peace?" Then tie your topic to this desirable thought. Phrases such as "Think how wonderful it would feel to . . ." and "In an ideal world, you would . . ." also lift the audience's spirits.

■ **Write what you see.** Like a reporter narrating a scene, create vivid "word pictures" to engage your listeners. Example: "The CEO settled into his plush office chair, typed in his password and downloaded his 72 e-mail messages. Then he rifled through the 48 phone messages his secretary left for him in a neat pile. Only then did he glance at the clock with a look of exhaustion. He was three minutes late to a board meeting."

■ **Adopt a fresh outlook.** Jerry Seinfeld built a career around making quirky observations about universal experiences, from brushing one's teeth to ordering in a restaurant. Borrow his approach to enliven your speech. Make provocative statements, such as "I've long been struck by something most of us take for granted" or "Within the next 24 hours, you'll probably lose something."

The perils of ad-libbing

Are you tempted to skip writing the speech and rely purely on ad-lib? Then you're setting yourself up for a fall. Observe others' presentations—good and bad. Speakers who ramble, lose their place, apologize constantly for being disorganized or crack dumb jokes to fill the time are the ones who undoubtedly figured they could muddle through without a hitch.

5 Secrets of Great Speech Writing

In his essay *Politics and the English Language,* George Orwell listed five rules of effective writing that apply to speeches:

1. Never use a long word where a short one will do.

2. If it's possible to cut a word, always cut it out.

3. Never use the passive voice where you can use the active voice.

4. Never use a foreign phrase, a scientific word or jargon if you can think of an everyday plain-English equivalent.

5. Break any of these rules sooner than say anything barbarous.

Smart speakers know what they want to say. They do not write out their speech word-for-word; they compose tight outlines and make notes to remind themselves of key points, quotes, stories, evidence or other must-include elements they might otherwise forget. As Winston Churchill said, a good ad-lib speech takes at least three weeks to prepare.

Realize that just as you might dread giving a speech, it's normal to hate writing it. Jotting down what you want to say can induce a fear all its own—it brings you that much closer to the jolting reality that you're going to stand in front of a crowd and actually go through with this! It's been said that writing is easy: You just sit at the computer and stare at the blank screen until beads of sweat drop from your forehead onto the keyboard.

The sooner you dive in, the better. All the research in the world won't do much good unless you assemble it in a logical sequence and outline your thoughts on paper.

Less is more

When it comes to word choice, adopt a less-is-more philosophy. Use as many one-syllable words as possible. Don't use a speech as a platform to show off your advanced vocabulary.

Consider these words from Nelson Rockefeller:

> *In 1960, they said I dropped out too soon. In 1964, they said I hung in too long. So, this year, I played it safe. I did both.*

Notice anything unusual? Every word has just one syllable, notes speech expert Joan Detz. While Rockefeller hardly enthralled crowds with JFK-like charisma, he wrote speeches that packed a wallop. It's hard to utter simple, punchy sentences like those above and *not* win over a crowd. Detz, author of several books on speech writing, also found that for the Gettysburg Address, Lincoln wrote 76 percent of it with words of five letters or less.

Cadence Counts

Preachers and politicians tend to appreciate the power of a flowing, rousing speech. But business people usually set a low bar in terms of writing rich, evocative and memorable presentations. They might repeat acronyms, spout buzzwords or recite reams of deadening data in a lifeless voice.

It all boils down to the audience's expectations. In most business settings, listeners don't expect an entertaining speech. And most executives do not attempt to use their presentations to captivate, unlock dormant emotions or awaken an audience's imagination. For a corporate speaker, there's usually an obligatory overtone that carries the underlying message: "I know you'll all pretend to listen, and I'll pretend this is important. So let's get it over with."

Yet if you want to stand out as a superb speaker, you must exceed your audience's expectations. How? Inject life and personality into your presentation. Engage people by making it easy and pleasurable for them to listen. Don't start by apologizing for the complexity of the topic or poking fun at your poor delivery. Instead, promise that you're going to delight listeners and give them valuable information that they won't find anywhere else.

Write your speech rhythmically. Just as in Chapter 1 we discussed the importance of organizing your ideas in threes, group words in threes as well. Lace your speech with triads that roll off your tongue and are easy for listeners to remember. In a speech by Franklin D. Roosevelt in 1937, cadence and balance combine to create a memorable sentence:

> *Here is one-third of a nation ill-nourished, ill-clad, ill-housed.*

Other examples:

> *Never was so much owed by so many to so few.*

> *We can ignore it, give up or fight to win.*

> *Our past stung, our present is uncertain, but our future shines bright.*

One of the easiest ways to enliven your speech is to vary the sentence length. Your average spoken sentence should contain 10 to 12 words. If you average 14 or more words, you're going to tax the listeners' patience. By alternating an occasional longer sentence of, say, 16 words with a short, declarative sentence ("This will not stand." "Talk about blind hope!" "Wait, it gets worse."), you dramatize your subject and keep everyone tuned in.

Another way to ensure variety is to pose rhetorical questions. Here are some particularly effective places in a speech to use a rhetorical question:

1. After a provocative or controversial statement, you can ask, "Do I agree?" or "Is that fair?"

2. To advance your speech, you can use a rhetorical question as a transition. Examples: "What next?" "Are we done?" "What's missing?"

3. After weighing all sides of an issue, you can ask, "So, what's best?" or "Which way to turn?"

Sentence fragments can save you from overdosing on long, convoluted sentences. When writing a speech, you can occasionally bend—and sometimes break—basic rules of grammar. For instance, a standard written sentence usually has a subject and verb. But when you're talking, you can reel off a series of short phrases that might look awkward on paper. For example:

> *The store struck me as odd. Poor lighting. No sign. Dirty aisles. A smell that I couldn't identify. Skunk mixed with sour milk, maybe.*

If you're going to speak in fragments, though, make sure each phrase builds on the previous one. Beware of repetition. This can occur if you let yourself get carried away when trying to make a point ("It was an outrageous offer. Just outrageous! Hard to believe! Just unbelievable!").

Also watch out for rehashing topics. You'll know you're going backward in your speech if you're starting every other sentence with "Like I said before . . ." or "As I said earlier . . ."

Finally, strike a pleasing cadence by stringing together parallel words or phrases in a balanced construction. This works especially well when you reel off a series of verbs. For example:

> *We must uncover new markets, delight new customers and welcome new teammates.*

> *By believing in ourselves, challenging our assumptions and tapping our reserves of strength, we'll be unstoppable.*

> *This investment poses credit risk, currency risk and market risk.*

When you write with parallelism, make sure you speak in a confident rhythm. Use voice inflection to punch out each verb with gusto (such as *uncover, delight* and *welcome* in the above example).

Plain English, Please

The more you research your topic, the more familiar you might become with technical terms or industry lingo. Even so, leave jargon out of your speech. Just because you understand an obscure or slang term doesn't mean everyone else will.

Lacing a presentation with complex terminology or overdosing on acronyms can turn the audience against you. They may resent having to translate your remarks into plain English.

Some speakers mistakenly think that because they know the technical level of their audience, the group will undoubtedly understand jargon. Yet the terms you might refer to in the office every day may sound inscrutable to your listeners when you utter them in a noisy conference room or auditorium. And all it takes is one person whispering to a neighbor, "What does *that* mean?" to trigger a roomful of rustling.

Assume that whenever you use an unfamiliar term, you cause at least a few listeners to tune out to make sense of what you've said. When they return their attention to your talk, they may have missed an important point. Or they may already have decided to tune out for good. Play it safe and speak the way you do at home, not at the office, even if the audience consists of many of the same folks you see at work.

Most people are better readers than listeners. That's one reason some dignitaries distribute copies of their speech ahead of time; they're proud of how it's written and they want the audience to read along. By avoiding jargon, you make it easier for everyone—whether they're reading or listening—to absorb every sentence.

In rare cases, however, introducing a bit of lingo into your speech can add pizzazz. Listeners often enjoy learning a new term that's gaining popularity. Just make sure you explain what you mean in clear, concise terms. For example, a financial adviser who mentions "EBITDA" can stop and say, "EBITDA might sound strange to many of you, but it's something that more and more investors will hear about. It means earnings before interest, taxes, depreciation and amortization."

If you're addicted to jargon or acronyms—and you find withdrawal too painful or stress inducing—then at least poke fun at yourself. Early in your speech, either show a slide with each of your favorite slang terms or recite them slowly and clearly. Then say, "By the end of my presentation, I promise that you'll become just as familiar with these terms as I am."

3.

Lights, Camera ... Rehearsal

*"We never do anything well
till we cease to think about
the manner of doing it."*

—WILLIAM HAZLITT
19th century essayist

"**E**veryone knows how to drink, so everyone thinks they know how to run a pub," says Khalid Aziz in his book, *Presentation Skills for Success*. The same goes with public speaking. Everyone can talk, so everyone thinks he can deliver a stirring speech.

When it comes to presenting, the biggest trap is the tendency to "wing it." You might figure you're too busy to practice, so you tell everyone within earshot that you don't have time to rehearse. You laugh and say, "I just hope they're a friendly audience" or "All I want is to get through it and get it over with."

Boasting about your lack of preparation is a sure sign of doubt and nervousness. Deep down, you fear you'll do a mediocre—even poor—job as a presenter. But you manage to convince yourself that the audience doesn't expect a magnificent performance; they just want to hear you and possibly gain something as a result.

That kind of attitude almost guarantees failure. Setting low expectations and then struggling to meet them means lost opportunities to win over your listeners. You'll muddle through, flubbing lines, forgetting your place, reading from slides and apologizing for this and that.

Practice Builds Confidence

Even the most gifted actors and comedians don't rest on their laurels. They rehearse their performances intensely. Since you probably lack the thespian talents of a Tom Hanks or Julia Roberts, that's all the more reason you should invest time in rehearsal.

The more you rehearse and free yourself from feeling self-conscious or awkward, the smoother your delivery. Practice breeds confidence. By familiarizing yourself with the material, sharpening your delivery, and anticipating mishaps and preparing ways to rebound from them, you'll radiate poise and self-assurance without even realizing it. The words will flow more easily, your facial expressions will seem more relaxed, and your gestures will create "word pictures" that enliven your speech.

Maybe a well-intentioned friend has told you, "Don't worry. You'll know more about your subject than anyone else in the room." That's one of the worst pieces of advice to give a speaker. Just because you think you know more than the audience has no bearing on whether you'll deliver your presentation with maximum impact. You still need to practice *how* you're going to convey your vast knowledge in the most digestible, comprehensible and entertaining manner.

Ironically, more seasoned speakers are often the most resistant to rehearsals. They may figure they've done it enough times so that they can coast, or they can draw on their experience to rescue them from any disaster. If this sounds familiar, you're sabotaging your success. While your years of speaking certainly make you better, that's no excuse to skip preparation and blithely hope for the best.

What's worse, many senior executives forgo practice because they assume their authority can save the day. They know they're not charismatic—and they glory in their low-glamour, deadening style. They may think, "I've made it this far without the rah-rah theatrics. There's no reason to change now."

Yet if you care about your message, you'll make every effort to communicate it properly. That means rehearsing it to the point where you're completely comfortable with both the content and your delivery.

Memorization vs. Planned Improv

Rehearsal does not mean memorization. Struggling to remember lines from a script almost guarantees you'll flub your speech. By focusing on what to say next rather than on how to connect with your audience, you'll strip the life out of your presentation.

Yet some speakers delude themselves into thinking that if they can memorize every line, they can't lose. So they wind up videotaping themselves as they read their speech verbatim, reciting it over and over in the mirror or clicking from slide to slide while repeating every word on the slide—as if that will somehow translate into a more captivating speech.

Here's the problem: If you memorize your speech, people will notice. They'll see your eyes darting around uncertainly as you try to think of the next line. They'll grimace if you suddenly stop and look terrified because you've lost your place. Or they'll shake their heads disapprovingly as you appear to push the words out of your mouth in a monotonous march toward a merciful end.

Consider how political candidates look during staged debates. A journalist poses a question. The candidate nods slightly—you can almost hear the mental wheels grinding. When it's time to respond, the candidate launches into a monologue that—aside from the first and last sentence that acknowledge the question—sounds completely canned. Such rigid memorization removes much of the spontaneity from the debate and makes the questions themselves seem virtually irrelevant.

In short, memorization enslaves you. You'll dwell on spouting preprogrammed phrases and become totally disengaged from the audience. You'll expend all your energy on sticking to a script, with nothing left to convince listeners you're talking to *them*.

So if you're not going to memorize, how should you maximize your rehearsal time? Talk through your topic in different ways. Practice citing your main points in a varied sequence. Mix and match examples and anecdotes. Quote experts, test stabs at humor and experiment by talking at varying speeds. By becoming vastly familiar with the overall structure and purpose of your speech and any interesting asides you'd like to toss in, the words will roll out of your mouth effortlessly when it counts.

Use your rehearsals for planned improvisation. Plant in your head the essentials that you learned in Chapter 1 (i.e., identify your goal, your three best points in support of that goal, and any stories or evidence you want to weave in). Then polish the way you express them to sound as conversational as possible.

To maximize your planned improvisation, activate a tape recorder for long sessions in which you hash out what you want to say and how you want to say it. If you're comfortable talking out loud with no one else around, that's often the

---

Exercise 2: Talk It Out

A great way to practice a presentation is to tape-record yourself as you answer the following questions:

1. What's the single most important overriding theme of my speech? What's the one big idea I want everyone to come away with?

2. How am I going to organize my speech? What are its three parts?

3. What are the most vivid stories I can tell during my speech? At what point should I tell them?

4. What are the best pieces of evidence I should mention? What's the best way to state this evidence?

5. How will I start my speech?

6. How will I conclude my speech?

After answering these questions, pretend to give the speech in small spurts. For example, say you answer Question 5 by saying, "I'll start my speech with a nice little story about how I stumbled across an old book in a yard sale that inspired me to build a business." After listening to that tape-recorded answer, hit the "Record" button again, but this time simulate giving the actual speech. You might say, "Four years ago while vacationing in Martha's Vineyard, the weathered spine of an old book caught my eye at a yard sale. I glanced at the title, *My Days and Nights as the Boss*. Little did I know that this obscure text from 1948 would change my life."

Befriend Your Slides

Beware of investing so much time in preparing the look of your slides that you skip rehearsing how to weave them into your speech. Don't spend hours experimenting with color schemes or font sizes at the expense of practicing what you're going to *say*.

It's fine to dwell on the design of your slides as long as you also consider how they relate to your remarks. That way, you won't read from them along with the audience as if you're discovering each slide for the first time.

Beware: When you say, "Let's look at the next slide and see what we learn" or "What this slide is saying is . . ." you'll put people to sleep. They'll conclude that you haven't rehearsed and are winging it.

Get to know each slide thoroughly before your presentation. Answer these questions in advance:

- *Why does this slide belong here?*
- *Why is it significant to my presentation?*
- *What should I say to the audience when it appears?*

most productive way to rehearse. If you prefer to have a friend on hand as a sounding board and critic, that's fine too.

The more you can practice vocalizing the key points you wish to make in the speech, the more confidence you'll gain. Any remnants of self-consciousness will fade as you keep hearing yourself sharpening your word choice, experimenting with the best voice inflection and perfecting your pitch.

Caution: As you listen and learn from these recorded practice sessions, don't turn into your own worst critic. Beware of convincing yourself that your voice sounds terrible, you're poorly organized, or your evidence is weak. Resorting to relentless self-criticism will immobilize you. Instead of finding ways to polish your presentation, you'll continually magnify minor problems and sabotage yourself.

Pass the Sound-Look-Say Test

Rehearsals work best when you know what to look for. By evaluating specific aspects of your presentation, you can plug holes and ensure that every dimension of your performance works to best advantage.

Some speakers practice religiously, but they don't know how to critique themselves. They may dwell on minor issues, such as whether their teeth look a bit stained when they smile, and ignore more obvious factors: their overall body language, voice tone and speech content.

For best results, rehearse your speech in front of a small group. Gather as many friends as possible to serve as your audience. Ideally, try to use the actual room where you're going to speak. Deliver the speech from beginning to end, and record it on video.

To set the stage for the most valuable rehearsals, take the *sound-look-say test:* Evaluate yourself based on how you sound (the audio), how you look (the visual) and what you say (the content). By finding ways to improve each of these areas, you'll leave no stone unturned. *(See box on page 28.)*

Woo a Tough Audience

Rehearsals can be dreadful if you're convinced the audience you'll face will be rowdy, restless or angry. By expecting the worst, you might psyche yourself out and inflate the threat that the audience represents.

The best way to rehearse for a potentially nasty or uncooperative audience is to anticipate problems and prepare to overcome them. Imagine what they're thinking and why they might object to something you say. Summarize their positions fairly, and practice stating their views in neutral terms. This will enable you to dignify their concerns and ratchet down their resistance when it counts.

Use these techniques to rehearse if you're going to face a tough audience:

■ **Highlight areas of agreement.** As you delve into controversial or sensitive subjects, begin by establishing common ground. List the areas in which you and the audience agree. Use phrases such as, "As much as we might differ over certain issues, many of you share my views about . . ." and "We may not see eye to eye about everything, but at least we agree that . . ." Practice speaking in a warm, welcoming tone to signal that you're reaching out in a sincere way, rather than spouting platitudes.

■ **Stage a Q&A session.** Enlist a friend to interrupt you with challenging or accusatory questions during your rehearsal. This will help you identify holes in your presentation. For example, if you're heckled about "playing loose with the facts" or "brushing over the truth," you can cite the source of your information and prepare a slide that shows supporting data. The more you can anticipate an audience's questions and objections, the sooner you can polish your speech to address those concerns.

■ **Experiment with diplomatic language.** As you rehearse, analyze your word choice. Avoid lacing your speech with sweeping judgments, stinging humor or snide remarks. Cut any comments that border on offensive. Don't use cynical phrases, such as "Of all the audiences out there, you people know best how to fudge the numbers" or "I don't need to tell this group about corruption." Even if you intend to be funny, such remarks can antagonize and polarize the audience rather than encourage them to lower their guard.

One of the benefits of rehearsing is that you can evaluate your speech from the audience's perspective. Stepping out of the presenter's role to consider the opinions of your listeners will boost your confidence and help you forge a connection with even the most stubborn groups.

Rehearsals also allow you to tighten your speech and speak more forcefully. Only by hearing yourself practice will you know if you're apologizing too much,

Exercise 3: 'Sound-Look-Say Test'

Below is an overview of how to rate yourself using the sound-look-say test. Use the questions as a guide when you screen a video of your rehearsal. You can also ask friends for critiques based on a printed handout of these questions.

Regardless of who does the evaluating, use a 1-to-10 scale, with 10 as the best score. Avoid letter grades (A–F) because people who might be reluctant to assign a D or an F will feel more comfortable assigning a 1, 2 or 3 to an area that needs significant improvement.

Sound:

_____ **Volume.** Do you speak at the appropriate volume so that everyone in the room can easily hear you?

_____ **Pitch.** Do you strike the right note so that your voice sounds soothing yet enthusiastic (as opposed to shrill, whiny or squeaky)?

_____ **Variation.** Do you vary your voice tone and volume to avoid a deadening drone? That means hitting highs and lows and perhaps inserting occasional shouts and whispers.

_____ **Inflection.** Do you emphasize the appropriate words in each sentence? Do you punch the word or phrase that conveys the most meaning so that listeners can understand you better?

_____ **Tempo.** Do you strike the right speed so that you're easy to listen to? Talking too fast can make your remarks unintelligible; talking too slow can bore your listeners.

_____ **Silence.** Do you use silence effectively to build drama, separate key points or allow the audience to "catch up" as you discuss complex issues?

Look:

_____ **Eye contact.** Do you look at individual faces in the audience for a few seconds at a time (as opposed to looking above them or avoiding them entirely)?

_____ **Gestures.** Do your gestures enhance your presentation by making it easier for listeners to understand what you say?

_____ **Facial expressions.** Do your facial expressions enliven your speech by conveying an appropriate range of emotions?

_____ **Clothes.** Do you dress professionally, with coordinated colors and complementary patterns?

_____ **Stage presence.** Do you seem at ease on stage? (Examples: If you use slides, do you stay focused on the audience rather than turn your back on them to read the slides? If you use a lectern, do you walk in front of it as necessary? Do you stroll the entire stage to get closer to every section of the audience, as opposed to planting yourself in one spot the whole time?)

_____ **Posture.** Do you stand up straight and command attention?

Say:

_____ **Flow.** Does every sentence build on the one before it so that you don't repeat yourself?

_____ **Evidence.** Do you support your assertions or opinions with solid, cogent evidence?

_____ **Audience involvement.** Do you mention audience members by name to break down the barrier between speaker and listeners?

_____ **Stories.** Do you weave into your speech concise, vivid anecdotes that reinforce key points?

_____ **Introduction.** Do you grab the audience's attention from the first sentence?

_____ **Conclusion.** Do you end by providing satisfying closure to your presentation? (Examples: a resounding call to action, a forward-looking expression of hope or high drama.)

adopting an overly defensive posture or subtly lambasting your audience's views at every opportunity. Control the urge to lash out or back down—that will make you a more commanding speaker.

Handling hecklers

If you expect your audience might turn into a band of belligerent hecklers, rehearse how you'll respond. Plan "spontaneous" comebacks that are face-saving and smart. For example:

- If they interrupt you to contradict your point, you could say, "We can play point-counterpoint all day." Then move on.

- If they fling a personal insult, say with a half-smile, "That's a good one. I like that." Then move on.

- If they yell, "That's nonsense" or "You're full of it!" say, "Please, don't mince words." Then continue.

Perfect Your Delivery

You want to sound dynamic, especially when facing a hostile audience that will pounce on any perceived weakness. Here are some rehearsal tips to improve your delivery:

■ **Condense your draft.** Although you shouldn't read your speech verbatim during rehearsal (or during the actual presentation!), you might refer to a rough draft as you practice. If so, beware of writing long paragraphs filled with wordy sentences. Instead, chop thick paragraphs in two. This will remind you to pause between paragraphs. Better yet, the text will look less dense and burdensome. Also scan your draft for overly long sentences: Cut three- or four-line sentences into two shorter ones. This will help you maintain breath control and pace yourself better.

Peter Giuliano, founder of Executive Communications Group in Englewood, N.J., encourages speakers to melt away "wax"—extraneous words or phrases that ruin the rhythm. For example, he would replace "This is absolutely and positively essential!" with "This is essential!"

■ **Insert lots of "you."** Count the number of times you say *you, your* and *yours.* Consider your rehearsal a success if you average one "you" for every three sentences. The next step? Train yourself to look into an audience member's eyes at every "you." By addressing them conversationally and making consistent eye contact, you'll impress even the toughest audiences.

"Without *you* on the page, a speaker may not look at the audience," warns Joan Detz, a presentation skills coach.

■ **Listen for fear.** As you critique a recording of your rehearsal, note any spots where you lose your poise. Examples include swallowing the ends of your sentences, rushing through your most powerful points and stumbling over your boldest assertions. Also, delete qualifiers such as "It seems to me" or "Now, this is only my opinion, but . . ."

Also prepare snappy one-liners to rebound from your own mishaps:

- If the slide projector bulb blows or some other technical problem occurs, look to the heavens and say, "It's a sign from above that I'm relying too much on PowerPoint."
- If you trip on the microphone cord or stumble on stage, say, "That was *so* hard to rehearse!"
- If you catch yourself making an embarrassing Freudian slip, shake your head in mock disgust and say, "Years of therapy, and look where it's gotten me."

Polish Your Timing

We've discussed the importance of rehearsing your speech by using planned improvisation, rather than strict memorization. That might lead you to wonder how to determine the length of your presentation if you don't recite it the same way each time.

Your safest bet is to set a range for the length of your speech. The upper end of that range should match the time that's allotted for your speech. For instance, if you're told to give a 20-minute presentation, make sure your run-throughs clock in at, say, 15 to 20 minutes.

There are many reasons to plan a speech that's slightly shorter than what audiences expect:

1. The actual presentation might take up more time than it did in rehearsals due to unforeseen glitches or your choice of ad-libs.

2. The risk of running overtime is far more serious than wrapping up early. Listeners resent a babbler who monopolizes the stage, thereby negating the substance of what's said.

3. Ending a bit sooner than expected gives your hosts some much-appreciated flexibility, which will surely endear you to them. Plus, you allow more time for the group to ask questions.

Always time your rehearsals from beginning to end. You'll find that deciding to tell an extra anecdote or adding another slide can lengthen your talk significantly. Beware of using the time for your first run-through as a final count. With each subsequent rehearsal, you may find that what began as a 10-minute speech can mushroom into 12 or 15 minutes.

When timing your speech, avoid stopping midway through and then stopping and restarting the clock. You won't be stopping and starting during the real thing. If distractions occur, talk right through them. The more authentic the feel of each rehearsal, the more benefit you'll derive.

Avoid trying to time your speech while practicing in front of a mirror. You'll get so caught up in the visual elements—your hair, facial expressions, posture, gestures—that you will talk at an artificial rate of speed.

Use your rehearsals to determine the best places to pause during the presentation. If you prepare a written draft, jot "pause" in red pen at transition points in your talk. Transition points include the ends of any sentences that:

• Complete an anecdote.
• Explain the significance of a specific piece of evidence.
• Carry the listener from one point to the next.
• Complete a quote or a citation.

Marking up your draft with reminders to pause not only enables you to deliver a more rhythmically pleasing speech, but also helps you gauge the length of your presentation more accurately. Consider that 10 pauses of three seconds each will add 30 seconds. After four or five rehearsals, you'll become so familiar with where to pause that you should no longer need to glance at your draft as a reminder.

Determine in advance whether you'll take questions from the audience. If so, work with the host of the event to decide how much time to allot to Q&A. If you're eager to engage listeners and launch a dialogue, then shorten your formal remarks to allow more time for group interaction.

10-Day Countdown

Some speakers figure that if they rehearse their speech once or twice a few days before the Big Event, they're all set. That's naïve. Follow this schedule in the 10 days before your speech:

✔ **10 days to go:** Finalize any props you're going to use in your presentation, the design of your slides and any special equipment requests for the room where you'll speak.

✔ **8 days to go:** Start allotting 20 minutes a day to rehearsing your remarks. How? Rather than read verbatim from a script, tape-record or videotape yourself giving an extemporaneous talk about your topic. Speak in a rich, resonant voice.

✔ **5 days to go:** Set aside the outfit you'll wear. Inspect every inch from head to toe to ensure your shoes are shined, your clothes are pressed, all buttons are secure, and there are no stains.

✔ **3 days to go:** Get a haircut or styling. Begin drinking at least six glasses of water a day to ensure you'll be properly hydrated when you take the stage, and reduce your caffeine and alcohol intake.

✔ **2 days to go:** Stage a complete run-through, preferably in the same room where you'll deliver the speech.

4.

Care and Feeding of the Voice

*"Most spellbinding voices were not born
of good luck. More often than not, they
are the product of a desire to learn."*

—Dr. Morton Cooper
Professional voice coach

In April 1992, Dr. Wilbur James Gould greeted a new patient in his office in New York City. The patient, who suffered from voice fatigue, gave lots of speeches as part of his job: running for president.

Dr. Gould examined the man's vocal cords and suggested steps he could take to regain command of his voice. The doctor's treatment paid off. The patient, Bill Clinton, won the presidential election later that year.

Clinton suffered from acid reflux, a common malady among executives who overeat and drink lots of coffee. As stomach acid flowed up his esophagus, his voice sounded increasingly thin and reedy. To make matters worse, while he was flying cross-country to campaign, Clinton would talk nonstop to reporters and aides. Dr. Gould and his colleagues warned Clinton that gabbing at 35,000 feet hurts the voice. Why? You must speak loudly to make yourself heard over the din, and the humidity in a passenger cabin usually is perilously low. Clinton's constant coffee intake (one staffer guessed he drank 20 cups a day, according to an article in *The New Yorker*, Oct.19, 1992) dried him out even more.

Under doctor's orders, Clinton began changing his lifestyle to protect his voice. He drank less coffee, lost weight, kept quiet on airplanes, observed designated "vocal rest" days, avoided smoke-filled rooms and even slept on an inclined bed to stabilize his stomach acid.

Prep Your Voice

You may never need to give dozens of speeches a day like a presidential candidate, but you must still take care of your voice. Blabbing on planes, depriving yourself of sleep or eating too much can sabotage your ability to deliver a rousing presentation.

Throughout this report, we mention the importance of voice tone and inflection. By striking a pleasing rhythm, you make it easier for listeners to understand you and believe in your message. Consider how Walter Cronkite earned the audience's trust with his authoritative downward inflection. Had he ended his sentences with a high-pitched squeal, we never would have believed a word he said.

You took the sound-look-say test in Chapter 3 to determine whether your volume, pitch, tempo and other vocal elements complement your message. Now let's examine the care of the voice in more detail.

Beat Back 'Frog Throat'

If you notice your voice is sounding increasingly froglike during presentations, resist the urge to clear your throat ahead of time. Each time you do so, you traumatize your vocal cords. It's better to clear throat congestion by swallowing, which may seem counterintuitive. But swallowing instantly helps you regain your voice and sound more authentic.

Hoarseness often indicates throat strain. If you tend to sound like you're gurgling, you need to improve vocal resonance by projecting your voice effectively. That means pushing air from your diaphragm—not your throat—as you exhale and speak. Experienced presenters use their throat to amplify their voice, not to produce sounds.

"Most people think the voice depends just on the throat," says Dr. William Riley, one of the voice trainers who advised Clinton in 1992. "But if you're stiff or out of shape, that will affect how you sound."

Riley finds that speakers who keep fit and exercise often tend to have richer, more resilient voices. If you're feeling lethargic or suffering even minor physical pain, it can influence how you address an audience. For example, hurting your ankle can lead to a less energetic or melodic voice. The same goes if you're wearing uncomfortable shoes or a shirt with a collar that's too tight.

Throat pleasers

Soothe your throat by treating your voice well every day. That way, you can deliver powerful presentations with the confidence of knowing your voice will work to your advantage. Some tips:

- If you talk on the phone more than an hour a day, beware of resting the handset between your shoulder and neck. Try a headset instead.

- Drinking caffeine or alcohol can parch your throat. Keep it moist by drinking lots of water, especially when you're on an airplane.

- Allergy sufferers: Taking antihistamines and decongestants can cause dehydration. Drink more water to offset the medication's effect on your throat.

- Don't get carried away at sporting events. If you must yell, hiss or cheer, use a hand-held megaphone to save your throat. Better yet, ration such outbursts or eliminate them entirely. (Of course, avoid yelling at your peers and employees as well!)

In the 12 hours before giving a speech, reduce your intake of dairy products. Gobbling a bowl of cottage cheese or a few slices of pizza might cause mucus

Exercise 4: Warm Up Your Voice

Even if you follow all the advice on how to protect your throat, you're still not out of the woods. You should also complete a series of pre-speech exercises to prepare your voice to sound its best. Obviously, you can't do warm-ups if you're waiting in the audience or seated on stage as a panelist, but beforehand you should run through the following exercises during your last few minutes alone:

1: The hum that refreshes

Hum in your normal tone for 30 seconds. Choose a favorite, relaxing tune. Then, for three seconds, hum a sliding scale that begins at your head and travels down to your chest. Benefit: This engages your lower chest resonance, which lowers the odds that your voice will crack or squeak during your presentation.

2: Testing your range

The most dynamic speakers tap the highs and lows in their voices. To identify your natural vocal range, find a paragraph in a book or newspaper. Start reading it aloud in a high voice. Then sigh slowly; at the same time, allow your voice to drop gradually to the bottom of its range as you keep reading.

3: Tongue flexes

The tongue is one of the most overlooked tools for presenters who want to speak with more definition and clarity. To improve your tongue's agility, double it back against your palate as far as you can. Then extend it outward from your mouth for three seconds. Repeat five times. *Alternate exercise:* Press your tongue against one cheek, then against the other. Now stretch it over your upper lip and let it fall so that it covers your lower lip. Waggle it from side to side for five seconds. Repeat 10 times.

buildup in your throat. Indulging in such foods prior to a presentation can clog your airwaves. Also pass up beverages loaded with ice; their temperature—often 40 degrees colder than your throat—causes the vocal folds to tighten and vibrate less freely.

Overcome Vocal Traps

Despite your impressive credentials, superb audiovisual aids and mastery of the subject, your presentation can fizzle if your voice sullies the audience's perception of you. A jarring or unappealing sound can divert listeners' attention from your content and cause them to doubt your credibility.

If you've heard your voice on tape, you probably think it sounds awful. That's normal. As your own worst critic, you might conclude that your accent is terrible, your squeaky whine is obnoxious, or you sound sick or subdued, not energetic and enthusiastic.

There's a reason you cringe when you hear your voice on tape: It's an entirely different sound from what you're used to hearing when you talk. Your skull serves as a resonator, so what you hear when you speak isn't what other people hear. Although this news might not sit well with you, the fact is when you hear your voice from an external source (such as a tape recorder), you're getting a more accurate sense of what others hear when they listen to you.

But don't reconcile yourself to having an embarrassingly bad voice. By ridding yourself of the biggest vocal traps, you can increase your power as a speaker. Speech coaches generally identify these pitfalls as the biggest threats to public speakers:

1. Mumbling
2. Nasality
3. Monotone

■ **Mumbling** poses the most problems for harried, nervous or unprepared presenters. They may dislike the prospect of public speaking so much that they rush to reach the end, stringing words together and swallowing the ends of their sentences.

Calm, rhythmic breathing reduces the need to mumble. Speakers who garble words often forget to breathe and, as a result, run low on air. By developing strategies to regulate air intake, you can speak more forcefully and clearly enunciate each word.

Sloppy breathing habits often result when speakers needlessly constrain their lung capacity. To enlarge your lung capacity, inhale deeply. As you exhale, count out loud starting from one. Keep counting for the entire exhalation. Leave about a half second between each number as you let the air out steadily. If your lungs are operating at peak condition, you should reach 20 before you run out of air. But if you struggle to get to 10, you need to improve your breath control. How? Take deeper, more deliberate breaths during the day. And pace your inhalations and exhalations so that you establish a slow, relaxing rhythm.

■ **Nasality** afflicts speakers of all ages and backgrounds. Morton Cooper, a longtime voice coach to Hollywood celebrities and executives, estimates that about half of Americans talk in a nasal tone that's too high-pitched. In a survey commissioned by Jeffrey Jacobi, a New York-based voice coach, 44 percent of respondents said the type of voice that irritated them the most was one with too much of a whiny, nasal quality.

If you speak in a nasal twang, it's probably caused by poor use of the muscles in your mouth, jaw and throat. When they're not functioning properly, your sounds won't resonate lower in your chest. Instead, you're apt to rely too much on your nasal passages to pump out the sound.

For Jacobi, reducing one's nasal pitch involves speaking with a more open, relaxed mouth and throat. He has found that certain vowel sounds pose the most problems, especially "ow" (as in "plow") and "a" (as in "candy"). To avoid nasality when saying words such as "now" and "cow," Jacobi suggests this exercise:

1. Drop your jaw and open your mouth wide, as if a doctor is checking your tonsils. Say "ah" repeatedly, making sure you can feel vibrations in your throat and chest.

2. Make the "ah" sound followed by "oo" as in "soon" or "woo." Repeat this "ah—oo" sound in one continuous exhaled breath. Begin each "ah" with your mouth open wide, and then round it out when you say "oo."

Jacobi warns that nasal speakers have the most trouble with words such as "mouth," "pound" and "count." That's because a whiny twang can develop whenever "m" or "n" precedes or follows the "ow" sound. He has clients repeat sentences such as "They're about to announce the amount" until they learn to speak from the chest in a round, open-mouth position.

By slowing your voice tempo and opening your mouth wider, you give air a better chance of exiting your mouth instead of your nose. That will lead to a steady decline in nasality. You'll also find it easier to breathe more evenly, which will in turn calm your jitters and improve your vocal control.

■ **Monotone** speakers tend to take shallow breaths and peel away the life from their remarks. Like an exhausted telemarketer, they may read verbatim from a script without passion or commitment.

One of the best ways to enliven your tone is to use a technique that speech coaches call "shading." That means enhancing a spoken sentence with an internal dialogue that induces you to talk with more energy. For example, you might begin a presentation by saying, "I'm Bill Smith," at which point you pause and say silently to yourself, "and I'm going to ace this speech." Then you say to the group, "For the last year, I've run a cross-departmental team devoted to finding new markets for our products," followed by this private message to yourself: "and you'll love what I'm about to say."

The problem with lifeless speakers is that they ruin any chance of success by feeding themselves negative internal messages, says Martha Burgess, a speech coach with a background in theater. You might begin by saying, "I'm Mary Jones," and then tell yourself, "and I hate being here." That almost guarantees you'll strike a deadening tone.

Control Volume, Tone, Tempo

The way you use your voice can largely determine whether listeners buy into your remarks or tune out. The best speakers know how to adjust their volume, pitch, inflection, tempo and tone so that others can easily understand what they're saying—and the spirit with which they say it. For example:

■ **Tell a touching story** by beginning in a normal volume. As you move toward the conclusion, speak more softly and slowly. This builds drama and conveys sincerity and poignancy.

■ **Arouse a group's passion** by starting in a low-key, conversational tone. Advance toward your call to action—your grand finale—by gradually speaking louder and reaching a crescendo at the end.

■ **Role-play like a pro.** If you're narrating a dialogue between two people, step into character when you speak their "parts." Like an actor playing two roles, modify your voice, stance and facial expressions when saying your "lines." Don't make a halfhearted stab at portraying different people—inject a theatrical flair.

■ **Relate key facts** in a slow, deliberate tone. When you want listeners to retain vital information, slow down! Enunciate every word. Adjust your volume one notch in either direction (slightly softer if you're talking loudly or vice versa) for added emphasis as you introduce new terms or ideas—or you want to call attention to your next point.

Example: Most speakers utter about two words per second, says Ronald Carpenter, a speech expert. During Gen. Douglas MacArthur's famous West Point address, "Duty, Honor, Country," he slowed his speed to about one word per second when he said, "My last conscious thoughts will be of the corps, and the corps, and the corps."

■ **Establish a rhythm** when you're running down a bulleted list from a slide or offering a series of examples. Pause just before you move from item to item to reinforce the fact you're going to a new point.

■ **Unleash your emotion.** One of the most revealing ways to differentiate seasoned speakers from novices is the amount of passion they inject into their remarks. Emotion and vocal range work hand in hand—the wider and richer your range, the more color you splash onto what you say.

Consider how Mark Twain reacted when he was dressing one morning and noticed a button missing from his shirt. He reached for another shirt, only to find a button missing from that one. Grabbing a third shirt, he saw that it, too, lacked a button. He started to rant and swear. Only after a minute did he see his wife standing at the door, giving him a disapproving look. In an effort to shame him, she repeated what he said in a slow, emotionless tone. He replied, "My dear, you have the words, but you don't have the music."

■ **Insert a one-second pause** between each point. This gives you time to think before you speak and increases the odds that listeners will heed what you're about to say.

Learn from books-on-tape

If you give frequent speeches, don't wait until the last minute to prep your voice. Whenever you can spare five minutes, play a passage from a book-on-tape that's read by someone whose voice you admire. Listen carefully to how the narrator enunciates, pauses and shifts tone and tempo. Now replay that same five-minute segment while reading from a printed page of the book. Don't try to mimic the narrator's voice. Instead, speak in your own voice along with the narrator. You'll soon learn when to pause, how to articulate tricky words and when to raise and lower your voice for full effect.

Above all, speak in an authentic, conversational voice. Don't sound fake by trying to mimic the tone of your favorite actor. Even if your natural sound works against you (especially a high, breathless voice), the solution is to modify your pitch and volume while staying true to yourself. Pretending to speak in a low, resonant voice will backfire.

It's wired into our brains to suspect speakers who put on airs. That's why audiences detect artificiality almost immediately. As long as your voice underlies your believability and sincerity, people will pay attention with an open mind. Your confidence will fill the room and induce everyone to listen.

5.

Briefings:
Make Them Clear, Concise

"My father gave me this advice on speechmaking: Be sincere, be brief, be seated."

—JAMES ROOSEVELT
Son of Franklin D. Roosevelt

Katharine Paine figured her briefing would be a breeze. As owner of a public relations firm and a former Hewlett-Packard manager, she was returning to HP's headquarters on a high. She expected to wow her old bosses—some of whom remained friends—by summarizing an innovative research tool she developed to measure the effectiveness of a company's marketing.

She began by asking, "How many of you have all the money you need to do all the things you want to do in your division?" That attention-grabber usually captivated executives. Not this time.

"I have all the money I need. That's not an issue," a senior vice president said. It went downhill from there. The others interrupted her mercilessly and challenged almost everything she said. Paine muddled through the briefing and fled in defeat.

Some of the hardest speeches to deliver occur in small rooms with just a handful of people in attendance. They may take only 3 to 5 minutes. The listeners, often bigwigs with little patience and lots of demands on their time, expect every word to matter. They don't want to hear funny jokes or long anecdotes. They need information—and they want it *now*.

When preparing a business briefing for their bosses, visiting VIPs, a board of directors or some other high-powered group, some speakers blithely assume they'll sail through just fine. They may think, "Oh, I know these people. Sure, they're powerful. But we've had lunch. We've played golf. At least they'll cut me some slack."

While all that may be true, don't treat a briefing as a casual, improvisational chat with friends. Just because you know—and perhaps like—the individuals, you still must prepare thoroughly, respect their time and deliver your points with speed, clarity and confidence.

Serve Small Portions

Most speakers who deliver briefings are vastly knowledgeable about their topic. That's a blessing and a curse.

When you know your subject inside out, you may want to throw in lots of asides, statistics or details. Trapping all those facts swimming around in your brain can prove almost impossible. You want to release them into the open, regale your listeners with your insight and show your expertise.

Your success in delivering a briefing to 10 or fewer people depends largely on your willpower. You must fight the urge to deluge your listeners with information they don't want or need. Stick to relevant facts, and move quickly toward your conclusion.

Think of a briefing as an appetizer to a meal. As the chef, you would want to provide a satisfying yet light dish, one that pleases folks on its own terms. If they suddenly had to leave the table after the appetizer, you would want them to say, "At least what I ate was delicious." The same goes with a briefing. As a result of your short, snappy, well-organized presentation, listeners should come away feeling that you valued their time and conveyed a clear message free of fluff.

To ensure you'll keep the briefing *brief,* map out your talk by stripping it down to its essentials. *(See Exercise 5: Five-Sentence Briefing on page 43.)*

Armed with a five-sentence road map of your briefing, begin with the premise and climb each rung of the ladder with speed and efficiency. Elaborate on each of your five key points for about 20 seconds. Come prepared to cite examples and evidence on request, but don't volunteer details or veer off on tangents.

"I've given thousands of briefings in my career and heard even more than that," said the late Admiral Elmo R. Zumwalt Jr., former U.S. chief of naval operations and a member of the Joint Chiefs of Staff from 1970 to 1974. "I've found the best ones are over in three minutes, and I can tell the speaker thought through exactly what needs to be said. There's a sense of direction. At its best, a briefing answers every one of my questions and addresses every one of my concerns in short order."

Play It COOL

Some speakers immediately latch onto the five-sentence format. They use this method to outline their briefing and guide them forcefully toward a conclusion.

Yet, depending on the topic and the audience, you may find it difficult to fit your briefing into a five-sentence road map. This often happens when you're dealing with a complex or ambiguous issue or you need to cover a diverse or unrelated set of points quickly. Fortunately, there's another organizational framework you can use that's ideally suited to more complicated, multifaceted briefings.

It's a COOL format in four steps:

1. Give the audience a reason to *care.*
2. State your *objective* or objectives.
3. Provide an *overview* of your findings, suggestions or observations.
4. Prepare *leave-behinds,* such as handouts or summaries.

Exercise 5: Five-Sentence Briefing

When you're addressing a handful of VIPs, plan exactly what you want them to take away from your remarks. How?

View your briefing as a ladder with each rung as a new point you want to implant in your listeners. Start at the base of the ladder with your opening premise, and build on it by assembling vital facts that lead toward your conclusion.

To fit your briefing into this tight format, streamline your message. Eliminate unnecessary or ancillary points. You'll know you've prepared well when you've reduced the body of your briefing into just five sentences. Below is an example.

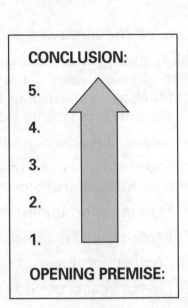

CONCLUSION:

5.

4.

3.

2.

1.

OPENING PREMISE:

CONCLUSION: We should hire a safety consultant, beef up HR and redouble our employee training and communication efforts.

5. We've received four anonymous complaints from employees about safety violations.

4. OSHA has notified us that it intends to monitor our safety practices.

3. We've repeatedly ignored our outside counsel's recommendations.

2. Turnover in our HR department was at 40 percent in the last year.

1. We've been hit with three employment lawsuits in the last year.

OPENING PREMISE: Our legal compliance procedures need an overhaul.

Remember this process with the words *care/objective/overview/leave-behind*:

1. *Give the audience a reason to care.*

Before giving your briefing, step into the listeners' shoes. Answer the question "Why should I care?" from their point of view. This will help you separate the details from the overriding issue or problem you're addressing.

Executives typically care about:

- Financial results or projected results.

- Stakeholders' concerns (whether those of employees, shareholders or other influential constituencies).

- Market opportunities.

- Potential or real crises.

- Competitive threats.

- Customer data (such as surveys, complaints, service delivery).

- Media coverage.

- Recruiting, training and motivating employees.

- Controlling expenses.

Once you've identified why your listeners should care, tell them in the first sentence. Introduce the core issue by relating a statistic, observation or experience that will grab their attention. For example:

- *In the last month, we've lost 15 percent of our best customers.*

- *Based on your comments about a marked increase in the number of returns we've processed in the last quarter, I've investigated the matter and uncovered some surprising information.*

- *Our experience with direct mail has taught us some expensive but critical lessons.*

When you begin with a stark, commanding statement, listeners will perk up and want to hear more. Plus, you gain clout as a speaker by boldly jumping right to the point. A captivating opening shows that you appreciate the listeners' concerns and intend to address them head-on.

2. *State your* objective *or objectives.*

Most executives sit through lots of briefings. They're often subjected to rambling speakers who either stray from the topic or harp on minutiae at the expense of larger, more important issues.

Prove you're well organized by stating the purpose of your talk in one clear sentence after giving your "why-you-should-care" opening. That way, listeners will know what to expect and be able to follow along more easily.

When presenting your objectives, emphasize each verb. Using voice inflection to underline the action words will make your goal even clearer. For example:

- *In the next few minutes, I'm going to **analyze** the data and **recommend** steps to improve our performance.*

- *My objective is to **list** three options, **weigh** the pros and cons and **suggest** the most sensible solution.*

- *I'm going to **present** strategies so that we can **pounce** on the current opportunity to **earn** market share.*

Keep in mind that stating your objective requires careful forethought. Don't assume your objective is so obvious that there's no need to articulate it. Lazy or unseasoned speakers tend to improvise. They might realize early in their briefing that they should state a goal to create the impression that they're organized, so they make one up on the spot.

When giving a briefing, you're responsible for guiding your listeners toward your conclusion with a minimum of fluff. Announcing at the outset what you intend to accomplish will boost your credibility and compel others to heed your remarks.

3. *Provide an* overview *of your findings.*

At this stage of a briefing, less experienced speakers get fooled. They might open expertly by giving listeners a reason to care, and then state clear objectives. But just when they're about to hit their stride, they digress or spout opinions.

To keep briefings short, you must summarize key points rather than elaborate on them. Give an overview and skip the details. Use phrases such as:

- *Here's what we've found so far . . .*
- *The study's highlights include . . .*
- *This issue presents us with three challenges . . .*

For many speakers, the hardest part of giving an overview is to resist the impulse to share everything they know about the topic. If they're briefing high-level executives, for example, they may want to impress them. Indulging their urge to show off or pontificate can sabotage their effectiveness and divert attention from the merits of their content.

The best overviews provide self-contained knowledge. If listeners were to hear only these one- or two-sentence summaries, they should come away with a strong sense of the speaker's overall message. For example:

- *Our analysis indicates that we must boost our return-on-investment on new technologies by increasing our testing, upgrading our current software and beefing up our internal info-systems team.*

- *In weighing the proposed merger, we confront three challenges: integrating diverse organizational cultures, cutting expenses while expanding our markets and selling our shareholders on the merits of the combined company.*

- *To take advantage of the changing market, we can launch a branding campaign, remodel our stores and pursue profitable yet untapped markets.*

How much should you elaborate? That depends on how long you're supposed to speak and how much information your listeners want. Find out ahead of time how much time your briefing should take. If you've seen other managers give, say, 10-minute briefings, don't assume you can follow their lead. Ask for guidance on its length from the senior person who'll be attending your briefing.

If your listeners demand at least some hard data as backup for your main points, you have a choice. You can either cite your support in the briefing or prepare a handout that they can take with them after your presentation *(see below)*.

4. *Prepare* leave-behinds.

While handouts can enhance any speech, they're particularly important when you give a briefing. Because you're often trying to squeeze lots of information into a short presentation, the materials you distribute at the end can build on what you say and reinforce key themes.

Yet the opportunity to leave behind packets of information can prove a double-edged sword. Beware of overdoing it. Just as every minute of your spoken remarks must count, every word in your printed matter must serve a purpose. Burying readers in reams of statistics will only aggravate and confuse them.

When it comes to leave-behinds, don't equate bulk with quality. Sift through supporting material and find only the most relevant data to distribute. Anticipate the questions or concerns listeners will have, and try to address them in print. That way, you can refer the audience to your handouts when they raise issues during the briefing. Or, you can give a quick answer and then add, "There's more information about this in the packet I prepared for you."

Examples of leave-behinds:

- A checklist of to-do items for the group to complete prior to the next briefing.

- Supporting details, such as a breakdown of survey results, customer profiles or case studies.

- Ancillary resources, such as Web sites, books or articles, for the group to conduct further research.

- A summary of key points you covered in your briefing in outline form.

- A CD-ROM, photo or product sample that illustrates something you described in the briefing.

Tip: Distribute leave-behinds at the end of your briefing. If listeners receive them as they enter the room, they might flip through the pages during your talk rather than pay attention to you.

If your handouts include a summary of your spoken remarks, let the audience know that at the beginning of your briefing so they won't feel the need to take notes. Some folks may still jot notes, but most will appreciate the chance to focus intently on your presentation.

Preparing a short summary also will help you stay on track. You'll know what you must cover and in what order if you've already committed it to paper. What's more, listeners will remember your points more easily if they can review them in writing later.

Engage With Eye Contact

Eye contact works wonders in any speech. In briefings, however, where you look and whom you look at often drive your success. Because you're addressing only a few individuals, you have a great opportunity to connect with each listener.

Before you begin, look at each member of the audience. Try to lock eyes with each person for at least two seconds. Many folks will greet your eye contact with a friendly nod as if to say, "I'm ready to listen."

But if they're fiddling with paperwork or whispering to a colleague, wait for them to settle down. Maintain a pleasant expression to show that you don't mind standing there a few more seconds. Don't sigh, smirk or roll your eyes. Your patience signals that you're a poised speaker who's not going to start until everyone's attentive.

In addition, your eye contact helps you connect with listeners. If you actually look at people, they'll feel you've customized your remarks for them. And they'll show more attentiveness in return.

Because briefings are so short, you need to use your limited time to include everyone. That's where eye contact helps. Look at the same person for two or three sentences at a time. Then find another for your next cluster of sentences. Keep moving from person to person, spending about 15 seconds looking at each of them as you talk.

Caution: Avoid "rabbit eyes"—hopping from person to person so quickly that no one really feels involved in your remarks. Looking at someone for a split second and then moving on does more harm than good; it makes the listener feel neglected. Talk to each individual long enough so that you'll feel comfortable redirecting your gaze to someone else.

Tip: If you feel you must read from notes, print the text only on the top half of the page. That way, you won't be looking down too far and showing the audience the top of your head. If you're going to print out excerpts that you plan to read to your audience, keep the margins of the text narrowly centered so that you won't have to move your head from left to right as you read.

Finally, use eye contact to integrate listeners into your briefing. If you refer in your speech to someone in the room, acknowledge that individual with a smile. Or, if you're proposing action steps or suggesting bold expenditures, look at your boss. The implicit message is: "I know I'm asking you to approve my plan, I respect you, and I want to make sure you and I reach an understanding."

Unlike formal speeches to a crowd of hundreds, a briefing lets you capitalize on the intimacy of addressing a handful of people. Your eyes can work to your advantage more than ever, so make every effort to forge visual connections with everyone in the room.

6.

Small Groups: Turn on the Charm

*"Is sloppiness in speech caused
by ignorance or apathy?
I don't know and I don't care."*

—William Safire
Columnist, *The New York Times*

Jerome Dodson, a portfolio manager for the Parnassus mutual fund, sometimes assigns his research analysts to make presentations about stocks they think Dodson and his fund should consider. In these small-group settings, Dodson and his colleagues will use the speaker's comments to decide whether to invest in a particular stock.

After one of his analysts delivered a speech about a company that recycles plastics, Dodson bluntly critiqued his employee's performance:

> *Your communication skills are lacking. You talk in a monotone, and you need to organize your material more clearly. You have a point of view, which is good, but you haven't done enough research or organized your material in a way that convinces me you're right.*

Dodson's comments, reported in *Smart Money* magazine (May 1996), unfortunately apply to many speakers who address audiences of five to 25. They often fail to tap the richness in their voice, organize their ideas persuasively or deliver a dynamic, memorable presentation.

When addressing a small group, you can make a lasting impression on each person in the room. The physical proximity between speaker and audience allows for more direct, unfiltered interaction. For example, by not using a microphone, you enable listeners to hear your voice naturally, without it being distorted by amplification. That adds a human dimension and creates more immediacy in how you relate to them.

It's also easier to read your audience at close range and adjust your presentation accordingly. Rather than look out over a sea of faces, you're able to see how individuals react to your remarks. You'll know when they're hanging on your every word or when they're growing restless.

Best of all, a small-group setting helps the audience bond with the speaker. You can engage everyone in your presentation by taking questions, exchanging quick asides and responding to their spirited nods, frowns or looks of disbelief.

The more you spur group involvement, the more they'll remember from your presentation.

Do Pre-Speech Interviews

With small groups, it's wise to chat with most, if not all, of the audience members before your presentation. Call or meet with those who'll be attending, mention the objectives of your talk, and solicit their input. Uncover the audience's expectations, needs and concerns so that you can address them head-on when it counts. Allotting five minutes per contact for, say, 10 people will take less than one hour. And you'll find every minute well spent.

By conducting pre-speech interviews with your audience, you can customize your presentation to ensure it delivers the information they want. Plus, you can refer to your listeners during the speech to humanize your topic. For example:

- *As Ted told me last week, he'll consider this session worth his time if he can come away with just one specific idea on how to develop more sales leads.*

- *When I asked Mary what she expected when she signed up for this, she said she hoped to get familiar with the latest technologies, the cutting-edge stuff.*

- *Almost all of you told me you didn't want a recap of last year's results. Ben, Chris and Jan were especially adamant that we should devote our time to looking ahead, not back.*

Set the Stage—Literally

When you're standing on an auditorium stage speaking to a crowd, you're bound to face distractions. Cell phones and beepers going off . . . babies crying . . . But for presentations to smaller groups, you can lower the odds of disruption by creating an environment in which it's easier to concentrate.

For example, if you see people entering the room with wireless phones, ask them to turn them off. If someone has a coughing fit as you're preparing to speak, you can provide some water. By being alert, you can spot potential disturbances *before* they derail your presentation.

The way you arrange seating can influence how the audience responds to your talk. When hundreds of people file into a room, they usually find standard theater seating, where they pick a row, squeeze into a chair and sink into anonymity. You can exert more flexibility when you're accommodating a group of 25 or fewer people.

After considering the room size and your objective in giving your speech, weigh these seating options:

✔ **U-shape.** Tables and seats arranged in a "U" often work best for small groups. Listeners plant themselves along the outside, and the speaker spends most of the time at the open end of the "U." This allows everyone to see and interact without craning their necks or moving their chairs. The speaker can stroll freely among the audience without straying too far from anyone or making certain folks feel excluded.

In using use a "U" configuration, you can signal what you want the audience to do based on subtle movements. Station yourself in the center of the open space for your opening remarks. To provoke discussion among the group, step outside the "U." By removing yourself from the group's line of sight, you send a silent message that you're going to withdraw and let them speak. When you want to reassert control, re-enter the "U" and the group's attention will instantly return to you.

Another benefit of U-shaped seating is the egalitarian spirit it introduces. Everyone in the group is equal. As the speaker, you command attention by standing while everyone else sits. But if you pull up a chair and join the "U," you create a democratic feel by being one of the gang.

✔ **Classroom.** If your listeners will take notes while looking at slides, props or other visual aids, they'll probably need to sit at desks or tables arranged in parallel rows. But when you position people in the role of student—and you're the teacher—you risk alienating them. Many executives dislike feeling subordinate to a speaker who doubles as an authority figure, and classroom seating can stir a bit of this resentment.

A partial solution is to have the tables arranged in a "V" pattern, with a central aisle running down the point of the "V." This adds informality and enables a small group to see one another more easily.

✔ **Theater.** Like classroom seating, the theater approach saves space but tends to drain the life from a small group of listeners. They're less apt to participate if they're bunched together looking up at a speaker on a raised stage. Avoid theater seating for groups of fewer than 50; for smaller audiences, choose a room that's less cavernous and geared more to interaction.

✔ **Conference table.** Some training facilities and meeting rooms are anchored by huge rectangular conference tables with swivel chairs dotting the perimeter. Listeners sit along the sides with the presenter at one end. This arrangement resembles the U-shape except there's no open space.

The conference table configuration can work well for small groups if your purpose is to educate them. One advantage of a large conference table is that each listener will have ample surface area to take notes, spread out exhibits, refer to training manuals or unfold maps.

As the trainer, you should plan on moving around the table while you speak. This way, you break up the monotony and encourage listeners to follow you around the room. As long as they're seated in swivel chairs, they should have no problem redirecting their focus as you roam. Also post flip-chart pages on the walls and walk to them when referring to points they contain. This keeps the visual stimuli flowing for the whole group.

Fend Off Interruptions

Small groups tend to pipe up. Listeners who would never think of interrupting a speaker in a roomful of hundreds will jump in freely with questions and comments when there are only 10 or 20 others in the audience.

If you're speaking to fewer than 25 people, expect interruptions. Prepare to think on your feet when you're heckled, challenged or otherwise thrown off track by outspoken people in the audience. The likelihood of disruption will soar if you raise contentious or sensitive matters that strike a chord with your listeners.

Anticipate at what point in your remarks the audience might cut you off. For example, some listeners may object to bold, politically incorrect statements or reject your attempt to cite controversial evidence. CEOs or other powerful folks might correct you if they hear something that rubs them the wrong way.

Once you've identified the most provocative points in your talk, think in advance of how you can silence interrupters gracefully. Prepare witty comebacks or assertive remarks that both acknowledge others' concerns and allow you to regain command and continue your speech.

Consider how a research analyst prepared a presentation to 12 of her senior managers. She anticipated the ruckus she'd raise by making blunt claims about the company's poor marketing, guessing that at least one person would defend the status quo or yell out, "There's more to that story!" So she rehearsed her response:

> *I realize my observation might ruffle some feathers, but I assure you that's not my intention. I want to assess our marketing plans by taking the proper perspective. I think you'll be pleased when you hear me out.*

In fact, when she started to discuss the firm's marketing mishaps, one of her listeners starting shaking his head and whispering to those seated around him. It became so distracting that the research analyst stopped her speech, looked at the man for about five seconds and then recited her prepared response. From then on, she wielded complete command of the group.

Don't look panicked

Disarm interrupters with a firm but tactful comment so that listeners can't derail your progress or detract from your authority. By knowing ahead of time how you'll fend off folks who blurt out their reactions, you'll gain the confidence to parry with a vocal audience.

Meanwhile, manage your body language to maintain your poise when others try to throw you off. Realize that the moment someone interrupts you, everyone else in the room will be watching how you react. They'll judge to what extent you're shaken. If you look panicked or caught off guard, you'll lose credibility. Your job is to hide your doubt, irritation and nervousness. Avoid excessive pacing, shaking or frowning. Make sure you're standing up straight and balancing your weight on both feet. Keep your hands away from your face so you don't nervously start massaging your scalp, pulling at your collar or fingering an earring.

Lock eyes with the interrupter—at least at first. This helps you send the unspoken message, "I'm still in control. You haven't broken my train of thought." Then respond quickly and diplomatically before picking up where you left off. At that point, shift eye contact to another listener at least a few seats away. This way, you remind all the others in the room that you value their time and want to ensure they stay attentive.

Take Questions in Stride

Even if listeners in small groups don't interrupt you with hostile cracks or criticisms, they might pepper you with questions throughout your talk. The intimacy of the setting can encourage your audience to raise their hands or blurt out inquiries whenever they feel like it.

Before your presentation, decide whether you want to field questions during your talk or prefer to wait until it's over. Usually, it's best to take questions as they arise, unless you're following a rigid outline or you must cover lots of critical details in a short time.

Allowing audience interaction also lets you know how you're doing. It's like getting instant feedback, a way to gauge your progress in connecting with them. Smart questions reveal that folks are listening and thinking about your remarks. The downside is that one or two individuals can harp on minor issues and prevent you from covering all your points.

If you're willing to take questions during your presentation, alert the audience at the outset. Say, "Feel free to raise your hand at any point if you have a question." When they speak up, follow these guidelines:

■ **Clarify the questioner's intent.** Before answering any question, know why it's being asked. Many audience members will explain their purpose in asking. They'll use phrases such as "Just so I understand you," "To clarify what you said," or "I'm confused about something." But if you're unsure why the person wants to know, say, "I'm not sure I understand your question." This invites the person to provide context or elaborate on the reason for the question.

■ **Tie your answer to what follows.** Lace your answer with references to what you're about to discuss. Say, "I'll expand on this later," or "I plan to cover that soon, but here's a sneak peek at what I'm going to say." If you don't intend to discuss the question in more detail later, try to link your answer to what you want to say next. Use phrases such as "This leads us to a related point about . . ." or "Another interesting aspect of this is . . ." That way, you weave the answers seamlessly into your prepared remarks.

■ **Admit what you don't know.** A risk of welcoming questions throughout your talk is that someone will ask something you don't know. If that happens, say so without losing your composure. Offer to investigate, confirm the right answer and follow up. Above all, don't improvise on topics you don't know much about. Once your mouth starts moving, you may find it hard to stop. What's worse, you might say something that exposes your ignorance or comes back to haunt you later. When you speak to a small group, audience members will be more apt to contradict you if they hear something fishy. That's all the more reason to say, "I don't know," rather than talk your way into trouble.

■ **Stall with a survey.** A luxury of addressing a group of 25 or fewer is that you can throw open a question to the rest of the audience. This is an especially useful option if you're reluctant to answer and you're looking for a way to stall. For example, if the question raises delicate issues or you need time to ponder the most appropriate response, look around the room and ask, "Would anyone care to comment on that?" or "What do the rest of you think?" You can even offer a menu of possible answers and ask for a show of hands so the audience can vote on their preferred response.

■ **Silence pontificators.** Some audience members will raise their hands and wind up spouting rather than asking a question. This tends to occur in small groups when listeners with big egos or senior positions in the organization feel obliged to make their presence felt. If a person opens with a string of statements that don't seem to lead to a question, jump in and say, "What's your question?" While you may not feel comfortable interrupting the CEO or a visiting dignitary, at least you can politely say, "That's an excellent point, and it certainly relates to the rest of my remarks."

Cool Down a Hot Audience

Just as listeners may feel more at ease interrupting you or blurting out questions, they might also flash their anger in a small-group setting, where they're less embarrassed to lose their cool. The physical proximity of the audience can make such confrontations even more harrowing.

Defuse an individual's anger by allying yourself with the rest of the audience. Rather than dwell on your antagonist's behavior, shift your focus to everyone else. Do they seem to agree with the irate person? Or do they appear ashamed, uncomfortable or sympathetic to your position?

Say an executive stands during your presentation and starts speaking belligerently. He gestures emphatically and points at you with an accusatory glare. Don't get locked into a one-on-one duel, which would exclude the other dozen or so people in the room. Instead, respond in a calm but firm tone:

> *If you could please return to your seat so that others can see, the audience would appreciate it.*

That allows you to become allied with the majority and shows you're sticking up for them. Better yet, it pits the troublemaker against the rest of the audience.

Similarly, if a rival manager wants to make you look bad in front of the top brass, he might feign outrage at something you say in an effort to rattle you. Don't fall into that trap. Rather than instinctively defend what you said, stay cool and say:

> *At this point, it's best if we stick to the agenda and cover all the ground that the audience has come to hear.*

That way, you cast your adversary as someone who is preventing the rest of the group from learning what they need to know.

7.

Large Audiences: Get Them Involved

"Great orators may be able to energize a crowd, get it fired up, sell ideas and foment revolution. But if the gift of gab is their only skill, they'll never make the grade. Glibness on the podium is less important than integrity and openness."

—Robert A. Lutz
Vice chairman, General Motors Corp.

Patricia Fripp gives hundreds of speeches a year. A longtime motivational speaker, Fripp realizes she cannot make eye contact with each person in a sea of 500 faces. So, to turn listeners into participants, she chooses her words wisely.

Her word choice pays off especially well when she tells stories. For instance, she used to say, "One morning I gave a speech to the IRS. After all, they get enough of *my* money." The line didn't elicit the kind of positive response she wanted, so she changed it. Now she says, "One morning I gave a speech to the IRS. They get enough of *our* money. I wanted some of theirs."

Similarly, Fripp has learned to involve the audience *before* she injects herself into her stories. She inserts a "you" sentence before getting to the "I." Fripp cites the example of a female speaker who starts off by saying, "When I was a cheerleader . . ." This opening sounds innocent enough. But it can alienate many listeners, who might resent a speaker bragging about that experience or might think, "My thighs were too fat to be a cheerleader." In any case, the audience feels shut out, annoyed or jealous.

A smarter opening builds rapport with the audience by taking their side. Example: "Have you ever been so embarrassed that you wanted the ground to open up and swallow you?" This causes most folks to nod and smile; they like the speaker already. Only then does the speaker enter the story by saying, "Let me tell you about when I was a cheerleader."

Talk Like a Visionary

When addressing a large audience, you must arouse their curiosity, win their trust and fill the room with positive energy. Within moments of starting your speech, you want them to think, "Good! This is going to be special." What's the easiest way to do that? Kill the rote "word of thanks," the boorish joke and the dull language. Talk like a visionary. Consider how Steve Jobs, chairman of Apple Computer Inc., opened a speech:

> *There are so many exciting things in our headlights that will take us through the next two to three years. Only after that will we start to send people out into the darkness.*

He doesn't just talk like a stolid CEO; Jobs marvels at the world. He paints an exciting visual image that makes it hard not to listen to what comes next. Like most great speakers, Jobs understands the expectations of his audience. He knows that Apple Computer has a reputation as a maverick and a beloved corps of followers. It's his job to talk like a visionary, to stir his listeners' imaginations and sustain their belief in his company's products.

Jobs wisely treats the audience as equals instead of trying to woo them by buttering them up. Similarly, Ron Shaw, CEO of Pilot Pen Corp., writes in *Pilot Your Life* (Prentice Hall, 2001), "Once you've made your entrance, launch straight into what you have to say. Don't dilute the impact of your opening with thanking your hosts or remarking how great it is to be in that city. Think of the first few seconds of a film. Would James Bond look into the camera and say, 'Good evening. Thanks for buying a movie ticket!'?"

Another CEO with a gift for addressing large audiences is Harvey Mackay, who founded Mackay Envelope Corp. in 1959. In his book *Swim With the Sharks Without Being Eaten Alive* (Ballantine, 1996), he advises speakers to answer 10 key questions before taking the stage:

1. Why did this group invite me to speak?

2. What is the group's purpose?

3. What are the chief characteristics of this group? (professional, social, demographics, career level, etc.)

4. Who spoke to the group recently? How were they received? Can I get copies of their remarks?

5. How can I personalize the speech for this group? What humor will work? What's off-limits?

6. Who are the opinion leaders in this group? Which of them will be there?

7. Who will introduce me? What will that person say about me? What should I say in return?

8. Will I take questions? What questions can I anticipate?

9. What messages will provide genuine "take home" value for this group? Should I prepare handouts, summaries, giveaways, etc.?

10. Who is my group "insider" who can help me develop my speech and give me reliable feedback on my performance?

Mackay's questions underlie the fact that when addressing more than 25 people, a speech gains formality. That's all the more reason to personalize your remarks and exceed the group's expectations.

Rise to the Challenges

Consider these challenges of presenting to large audiences:

■ **The physical distance** between speaker and listener is usually greater than in a small-group setting. The speaker may appear on a raised stage and tower over the audience, transforming them into passive, potentially daydreaming drones.

■ **The use of a microphone** can distort the speaker's natural voice; words such as "pepper" and "planning" can create a popping sound that jars the audience.

■ **If a speaker fails to enthrall** everyone from the outset, pockets of listeners may whisper among themselves or simply walk out.

As a result, you've got a series of obstacles to overcome when you're addressing the masses:

- Pierce the veil of formality to breathe life into your speech and communicate in an engaging manner.

- Conquer your fear of crowds so that you stay poised even if you flub a line or confront a heckler.

- Speak in a voice tone and volume that make it easy for everyone in every part of the room to hear you.

- Control your body language so that you appear confident and avoid distracting gestures.

- Spread your eye contact to individuals around the room so no one feels neglected.

This chapter will give you strategies to win over large audiences by gaining awareness of how you speak, move and act when you're on stage. While there's no way to rid yourself of all traces of nervousness, you can develop ways to establish a commanding presence and carry your audience along for an enjoyable, stimulating and informative presentation.

Show You Know the Audience

Imagine you're sitting amid 100 or more people as a speaker springs onto the stage. You think, "I hope this is worth my time." Within 30 seconds, you have your answer. The speaker captures your interest, wins your respect and appears earnest, smart and well organized. You're hooked.

Now imagine you're the speaker. How did you engineer such a smooth, winning, credibility-building introduction?

For starters, you gauged the knowledge level of your audience and struck exactly the right tone in addressing them. You did this by researching the group ahead of time, as we discussed in Chapter 2. You didn't open by asking for "a show of hands" after asking, "How many of you have . . . ?" or "Do you have experience with . . . ?"

Some misguided speakers survey large audiences to determine how much detail they should provide or whether they need to define certain terms. That's a mistake. These speakers may assume that if only a few people raise their hands, then they must step back and give a wordy overview of the topic, along with a summary of its importance to the group. Only then will they segue into their planned presentations.

While that approach may sound flexible and effective in theory, it often backfires in practice. Many people refuse to raise their hands. They may prefer to sit still and detach themselves from the proceedings, feeling annoyed or demeaned by the speaker's antics.

Skip the show-of-hands silliness. Instead, demonstrate your familiarity with the audience. Here's how:

■ **Share your field research.** Cite past comments from audience members and how they've influenced what you're going to cover. Example:

> *Over the last week, I've spoken to about 10 of you regarding how I should approach this presentation. I tried to pick folks who would provide an accurate sampling of the entire group. Here's what I learned . . .*

■ **Appeal to universal experiences or emotions.** Refer to big-picture themes or common bonds that bring everyone together. Example:

> *We all come from different backgrounds and probably hold somewhat strong opinions about what this company has done right and wrong. But here's one thing we all share: We care.*

■ **Cite demographic data.** Provide a demographic breakdown of your audience. If you serve as guest speaker, ask the host ahead of time to give you information on your audience, such as gender, job title/description, experience in their field and years of membership in the sponsoring organization. By weaving this data into your speech, you provide a thumbnail sketch of your audience, which they'll undoubtedly find interesting.

Speak the Silent Language

People will judge you from the moment you enter the room. They'll notice your facial expression, how you walk toward the podium and how you're dressed. Send the right nonverbal signals, and you'll have the audience on your side from the very beginning.

Most listeners care more about a speaker's behavior and voice tone than the content itself. If you stand with your feet comfortably apart, weight distributed equally on the balls of both feet and your shoulders relaxed (not hunched), you will command attention before uttering a word.

When standing in front of a big crowd, your body language matters more than ever. The audience may not listen intently to your every word, but they'll probably *look* at you the whole time. They expect to see someone who stands up straight, radiates confidence and gestures effortlessly and naturally. If your hands are shaking nervously or you keep taking off your eyeglasses every few minutes, your movements will detract from your message.

Audiences will follow your nonverbal lead. When you look confused or annoyed, they'll wonder what's going on and probably feel somewhat peeved, too. If you're distracted, don't show it. Always strive to appear in control—*even when you're not*. If you notice a VIP leaving the room in a huff or you sense some hub-bub in the back of the room, don't frown or stare. Why? Everyone else will turn around to see what's going on, and you'll lose any bond you've established with the audience.

A subtler but equally distracting problem with body language occurs when speakers lapse into repetitive or unnecessary gestures. Rather than use their hands, arms and shoulders to fullest advantage, they might slap at the air repeatedly or spin their hands in constant circles like a football referee signaling that the game clock's still running. While there's nothing inherently wrong with these gestures, you can overdo it. Just because you lose track of your gestures, your audience won't. A good rule of thumb: *Move only when you have a reason to move.*

To develop a wider range of body language, practice your speech without using any gesture more than once. Videotape yourself, and track each distinct hand or body motion to ensure you don't resort to the same ones over and over again.

When the time comes to deliver your presentation, create an "anchor position" with your hands resting comfortably at your sides. Don't clasp them behind your back or in front of you in a fig-leaf pose. And don't clutch a pen or index card; keep both hands free of any objects.

As you approach the podium, make friends with your body. Relax your arms, drop your shoulders and loosen your facial muscles. Imagine you're standing amid a circle of friends at a party, where your facial expressions and body movements enliven your remarks and add zest to your personality. Now apply that in front of an audience: Open the floodgates and let your enthusiasm flow forth for all to see.

Make jumbo-sized gestures

If you're addressing a group of 200 or more, gestures take on even more meaning. People seated in the back of the room may not see every subtle shift of your facial expression, but they'll surely pay attention when you lift both your hands above your head in a wide, expansive gesture (perhaps while saying, "It was like the weight of the world came crashing down on my shoulders"), or you extend both outstretched palms plaintively toward the audience (perhaps while asking, "Tell me, what did I do wrong?").

To reinforce your message in front of a crowd, hold your gestures and facial expressions an extra second or two. That makes them easier for everyone to see. For example, when you put your arm out, extend it all the way out and keep it there until you've completed your point. If you raise your hand, lift it all the way

> ## Give Your Hands, Arms a Rest
>
> Some of the most expressive gestures need not involve your hands or arms. Here are three examples of underused nonverbal cues:
>
> ■ **The head tilt.** Since he was paralyzed, Franklin D. Roosevelt needed to grip the lectern to hold himself up, so he could not wave freely. As a result, he often tilted his head to one side while speaking to large audiences. Coupled with his facial expressions, Roosevelt's head tilts could convey confidence, skepticism, thoughtfulness or sadness.
>
> ■ **The bold step.** Aimless pacing can make you look like a criminal killing time in a prison cell. But if you take a few strides at critical junctures in your speech, you signal to your audience that you're about to say something important. For example, you can start speaking from behind a lectern and then step in front of it after your introduction. If you're not using a lectern, you might take two or three steps toward the audience as you transition from telling a background anecdote to your main point.
>
> ■ **The smile.** When you're genuinely excited or pleased, an ear-to-ear smile can delight your listeners. Beaming occasionally can prove contagious. It fills the room with positive energy and makes the audience more receptive to your message.

up. This will keep you from making halfhearted, jerky gestures, which would sabotage your stage presence.

Tip: Gestures must flow naturally from your remarks. If they look canned or rehearsed, they'll backfire. As you watch videotapes of your presentation and become familiar with your gestures, identify the ones that look the least forced and most engaging. These can become your signature moves, the nonverbal ways you express emphasis and paint word pictures.

Charismatic speakers look like they're enjoying themselves. They flash a natural smile at just the right moment. Then they turn serious and speak from the heart. They don't just scan the audience; they actually look into a listener's eyes in a sincere, friendly manner. They use their whole body to make a point, wiggling briefly from side to side to communicate excitement or putting their hands on their hips momentarily in a playful attempt to scold the audience. They'll pump a fist in the air to signify victory, and the audience will love them for it.

Make Allies in the Back Row

In a roomful of people, it's tempting to concentrate on the folks seated closest to you. This tends to happen when:

- Your friends or dignitaries sit in the front row, and you devote most of your eye contact to them.

- You're intimidated by the sheer size of the audience so you talk only to people in the first few rows.

- The lighting is best in the front of the room so you look at only those nearby whom you can see.

Disregard listeners in distant rows at your own risk. They'll notice almost immediately if you refuse to look in their direction—and they'll tune out. In an audience of 200, you might alienate 170 of them by failing to look at them and to acknowledge their presence. Their rustling and whispering, in turn, can distract the folks in the front rows who are trying to pay attention to you.

Just before beginning your speech, make eye contact with someone in the back row. This "visual embrace" alerts faraway listeners that you're not going to forget them. If you notice in the moments before taking the stage that poor lighting will make it hard for you to see into the distance, ask an aide to adjust the brightness to save you from squinting.

Aside from eye contact, one of the best ways to involve the back row is to make sure they can hear you. The larger the room, the longer it takes for your voice to carry to the far corners. That's why you should not only test the microphone in advance to confirm everyone will hear you, but also observe the behavior of back-row listeners in the first minute of your presentation. If they laugh at your opening anecdote, that shows they can hear you. But if they look annoyed or confused, that might mean your voice isn't reaching them. Finish your sentence and ask, "Can everyone hear me in the back?" Use their feedback to adjust the microphone, talk louder or, as a last resort, ask individuals seated farthest away to move up and fill empty seats closer to the front.

Big crowds also appreciate speakers who vary their voice tone. A little theatrics can go a long way. Examples include whispering when you want to inject a conspiratorial element into your remarks and raising your voice to express surprise or mock anger. If you're rallying the group to believe in your cause, let your voice build to a crescendo: Start softly and turn up the volume as you gather momentum and guide everyone toward a rousing conclusion.

Watch your tempo as well. Nervous speakers tend to rush through their speech, stringing words together indecipherably. Rattling on at a rapid clip almost guarantees no one will follow what you say. The solution is easy: Slow down. Use John Wayne as an inspiration. He once told a reporter that the secret of his dis-

Overcome 'Pain of the Pause'

Only you feel awkward when you pause during a speech. In a big audience, the crowd welcomes such brief silences. They might cough, adjust their seats or reach for a pen in their briefcases. Speakers should not "give in to the pain of the pause," says Kevin Daley, president of Communispond, a New York-based speech coaching firm. While you suffer, the audience is admiring your confidence and control!

tinctive delivery was that he cut each sentence in half: He said the first half, stopped, then said the rest. While you shouldn't pause at the midpoint of every remark, of course, pause frequently to collect your thoughts, build drama and help the audience understand you.

Own the Room

When you're standing in front of hundreds of eyeballs, planning takes on even more importance. Slides and props must be easy for everyone to see; you must look and feel at ease; lighting must work to your advantage.

In the days before your speech, you should become well acquainted with the room in which you'll speak. "Survey the venue well before you're on," says Patrice Carroll, vice president of MCI WorldCom. "Find out about backdrop. If it clashes with your clothes, you will not be a pleasant sight. Also, look to see if there are any cords that may be in your path."

Know every foot of space you have to work with. Listen for creaky boards, air-conditioning hums or backstage noises that might compete with your remarks for the audience's attention. Look for ground wires, loose or slanted flooring, stairs or other potential perils that might pose an obstacle course during your speech. Take note of any beams, large plants or other objects that can block the line of sight between you and certain segments of the audience.

On the day of your presentation, check out the room at least an hour ahead of time. Bring along an aide to test the range of the microphone by sitting in different parts of the room and giving you feedback. That's the best way to gauge the acoustics and determine how well your voice carries.

In terms of lighting, make sure you'll be able to look your listeners in the eyes. Beware of auditoriums where the audience sits in the dark while bright lights bathe the stage. You'll spend the whole speech squinting and wishing you could connect with people visually. Arrange with your hosts to maintain sufficient lighting to fill the whole room.

If you're going to show slides, dim the lights as needed, but don't throw the audience into pitch-blackness. People tend to get sleepy or inattentive when they're seated in a dark room.

Review with the stagehand how and when certain lights will be dimmed during your presentation. Make sure they put masking tape over any dials or switches that you do *not* want touched. That lowers the odds someone will flip the wrong switch at the worst possible time. Use tape to denote where on the podium the lighting begins and ends so you will know where not to step out of the spotlight.

Decide in advance how you're going to distribute your eye contact so that you engage everyone in the room. Victoria Chorbajian, a speech coach in Paramus, N.J., suggests that when addressing more than 25 people, a speaker should establish at least three "eye-contact points." By picking three spots in various parts of the room, the speaker is forced to look at different clusters of listeners. Chorbajian warns that ineffective speakers might have only one eye-contact point—a friendly face whom they latch onto early in the speech and never let go.

Rehearse Your Walk to the Stage

Audiences love to render first impressions of a speaker. They'll judge you from the moment they see you. That's why you should rehearse exactly how you'll stride to the stage. If someone's introducing you, decide in advance if you'll shake hands, hug or exchange a few quick remarks. Plan where you'll both stand when you greet each other so there won't be any last-minute vying for position.

If you're going to approach the podium from the audience, practice walking at the appropriate speed. Don't bound onto the stage like a crazed game-show host. Racing to the lectern will only trigger a more rapid heartbeat, making you feel even more nervous. It's better to walk toward the front of the room at a somewhat slow, controlled pace.

Also, don't fumble around at your seat or plant yourself in the middle of a long row of folks who must scoot aside while you fight your way out. If it takes you too long to get up to the stage, you'll test the audience's patience.

Design Slides Everyone Can Appreciate

When you address dozens of onlookers, slides can provide a much-needed crutch for you. But while effective slides can make your content come alive, they can also put people to sleep.

The minute you dim the lights to show the first image, you'll notice that some folks will recline in their seats and virtually doze off. Even if they try to remain alert, it's hard to fight the passivity that sets in when they sense the speaker has shifted into a lifeless "let's-get-through-these-slides" mode.

What's worse, some speakers rely on slides to drive their speech. They don't bother to make eye contact with their listeners or interact with them. Instead, they hop from slide to slide in a mechanical drone.

Yet, at their best, slides can boost a speech's impact. Many speech coaches claim that a well-designed visual aid can raise audience retention of the content by 30 percent to 40 percent. For instance, reciting percentages of your marketing budget devoted to advertising, PR, winning new customers and keeping the current ones won't work nearly as well as showing a pie graph of the budget breakdown in more simple, visual terms.

The mid-1990s introduced presenters to multimedia software programs that make it easy to design snazzy slides. PowerPoint, the most popular such tool, has largely replaced 35-mm slides and overhead transparencies. You can add animation, scanned images, sound and video when using new media. Computer-generated slides arouse the senses and provide visual appeal in ways that old-fashioned slides or writing on an easel cannot.

At the same time, however, presenters can overdo it today. It's easy to pack PowerPoint slides with too much information. Fancy graphics can outshine the speaker and leave the audience confused and exhausted from sensory overload. "Don't use PowerPoint and other multimedia crutches," says Guy Kawasaki, CEO of garage.com, in an interview in *Forbes ASAP* (Aug. 23, 1999). "This stuff seldom works right. Even if you get the thing running, you'll have too much text in too small a font size."

While you may find it hard to resist PowerPoint entirely, use these pointers to design appropriate slides for a large audience:

■ **Strive for simplicity.** No slide should consist of more than 40 words. List concise bullets; limit each line to seven words or less. If you're resorting to lots of punctuation—commas, dashes and semicolons—that's a bad sign. You don't want to adopt a chatty tone or write run-on sentences. Skip footnotes and source lines that clutter the image. Also, choose your bullets judiciously; never have more than seven bulleted items on one slide.

■ **Choose legible type.** Audience members seated farthest away must be able to see the slide easily. Variables such as projector brightness and color contrast can affect the clarity of the image. Gene Zelazny, author of *Say It With Presentations* (McGraw-Hill, 2000), shows how far from the screen someone can sit and still read a slide:

<u>**Maximum Distance From Screen**</u>

Size of type	Width of screen		
	6 feet	**8 feet**	**12 feet**
16 pt. lowercase	15 feet	18 feet	20 feet
18 pt. lowercase	23 feet	25 feet	27 feet
20 pt. lowercase	30 feet	35 feet	45 feet
22 pt. lowercase	35 feet	40 feet	50 feet
24 pt. lowercase	45 feet	50 feet	60 feet
30 pt. lowercase	50 feet	60 feet	70 feet
32 pt. lowercase	62 feet	70 feet	80 feet

■ **Think "less is more."** Just because you can incorporate sound or animation into your slides doesn't mean you should. Use special effects sparingly. Make sure they enhance your content rather than muddy it. The same goes with color: Stick to a simple, consistent color scheme rather than integrating dozens of pixel variations into your slides.

■ **"Brand" your slides.** Run a border along each slide with branding basics, such as your company's logo and Web address. This will make it easier for your audience to follow up with you.

■ **Root out technical glitches.** Arrive early and test all the multimedia equipment you're going to use. Examples: Confirm that audio and video playback and software work in tandem, all cables are properly connected, and you'll have unimpeded Internet access during your presentation.

Get to know the technician assigned to help you set up for your speech. Find out how you can signal this person quickly if you run into technical difficulties during the presentation. Know this person's whereabouts at all times.

In terms of lighting, surround the screen in sufficient darkness so that the images are easy to see from far away. But maintain enough light where the audience sits so they can see their materials and take notes. Also, beam plenty of light onto yourself so that people can still see you.

You read in Chapter 3 that you shouldn't read from your slides along with the audience. That would almost guarantee you'd shut down any chance for dialogue and divert listeners' attention from your presentation. You want everyone to focus on you, not on your slides.

Weave in Slides With 3 T's

Many presenters misuse their slides. They rush from image to image without allowing the audience to analyze each graphic. Pace yourself by using the *turn-take-talk* method:

Turn toward a new slide or flip chart as it becomes visible to the audience. But don't swing around entirely, with your back to the audience; simply rotate 90 degrees so you can glance at the graphic.

Take two seconds to review the graphic. Silently remind yourself of the most important point you want the audience to extract from that image.

Talk. Re-establish eye contact with the audience. Then make a provocative comment about the slide, such as "What's surprising here is . . ." or "Notice the high number of . . ." Keep your eyes on the audience. Turn back to the image with a pointer only after you've addressed the audience directly for about five seconds.

Appendix: Resources

Magazines/Newsletters

Presentations. Monthly magazine that provides how-to articles on using teleconferencing equipment, PowerPoint and other presentations software. (800) 707-7749; *www.presentations.com.*

The Executive Speaker. Monthly newsletter with speech-writing tips. (937) 294-8493; *www.executive-speaker.com.*

Books

The Presentations Survival Skills Guide by Scott Lee (Distinction Publishing, 2001).

Last-Minute Speeches and Toasts by Andrew Frothingham (Career Press, 2000).

PowerPoint 2000 Professional Results by Ellen Finkelstein (McGraw-Hill, 1999).

Effective Executive's Guide to PowerPoint 2000 by Stephen L. Nelson and Michael Buschmohle (Redmond Technologies, 2000).

Creating Dynamic Multimedia Presentations Using Microsoft PowerPoint by Carol M. Lehman (South-Western Publishing, 2000).

PowerPoint 2000 by Michael Miller (Sybex, 2000).

Web Sites

www.abacon.com/pubspeak/

The Allyn & Bacon Public Speaking site provides comprehensive information on public speaking, along with tips on using the Internet for research. The last of its five-part module on speech preparation covers when and how to use multimedia tools to best effect.

www.sayitbetter.com

This site includes Kare Anderson's hints on using nonverbal cues.

www.toastmasters.org

In addition to the tips found on its Web site, Toastmasters International has thousands of local clubs for speakers who want to polish their skills.

www.webofculture.com/worldsmart/gestures.asp

Roger Axtell, author of *Gestures,* has excerpts from his book on body language in different cultures.

AQUAMAN

VOL.3 CROWN OF ATLANTIS

AQUAMAN
VOL. 3 CROWN OF ATLANTIS

DAN ABNETT
writer

SCOT EATON * **PHILIPPE BRIONES**
BRAD WALKER
pencillers

WAYNE FAUCHER * **PHILIPPE BRIONES**
ANDREW HENNESSY * **SCOTT HANNA**
inkers

GABE ELTAEB
colorist

PAT BROSSEAU
letterer

BRAD WALKER, ANDREW HENNESSY
& GABE ELTAEB
collection cover artists

AQUAMAN created by **PAUL NORRIS**

BRIAN CUNNINGHAM, ANDY KHOURI Editors - Original Series ⚫ **HARVEY RICHARDS** Associate Editor - Original Series
AMEDEO TURTURRO, DIEGO LOPEZ Assistant Editors - Original Series
JEB WOODARD Group Editor - Collected Editions ⚫ **LIZ ERICKSON** Editor - Collected Edition
STEVE COOK Design Director - Books ⚫ **SHANNON STEWART** Publication Design

BOB HARRAS Senior VP - Editor-in-Chief, DC Comics

DIANE NELSON President ⚫ **DAN DiDIO** Publisher ⚫ **JIM LEE** Publisher ⚫ **GEOFF JOHNS** President & Chief Creative Officer
AMIT DESAI Executive VP - Business & Marketing Strategy, Direct to Consumer & Global Franchise Management
SAM ADES Senior VP - Direct to Consumer ⚫ **BOBBIE CHASE** VP - Talent Development
MARK CHIARELLO Senior VP - Art, Design & Collected Editions ⚫ **JOHN CUNNINGHAM** Senior VP - Sales & Trade Marketing
ANNE DePIES Senior VP - Business Strategy, Finance & Administration ⚫ **DON FALLETTI** VP - Manufacturing Operations
LAWRENCE GANEM VP - Editorial Administration & Talent Relations ⚫ **ALISON GILL** Senior VP - Manufacturing & Operations
HANK KANALZ Senior VP - Editorial Strategy & Administration ⚫ **JAY KOGAN** VP - Legal Affairs
THOMAS LOFTUS VP - Business Affairs ⚫ **JACK MAHAN** VP - Business Affairs
NICK J. NAPOLITANO VP - Manufacturing Administration ⚫ **EDDIE SCANNELL** VP - Consumer Marketing
COURTNEY SIMMONS Senior VP - Publicity & Communications
JIM (SKI) SOKOLOWSKI VP - Comic Book Specialty Sales & Trade Marketing
NANCY SPEARS VP - Mass, Book, Digital Sales & Trade Marketing

AQUAMAN VOL. 3: CROWN OF ATLANTIS

Published by DC Comics. Compilation and all new material Copyright © 2017 DC Comics. All Rights Reserved.
Originally published in single magazine form in AQUAMAN 16-24. Copyright © 2017 DC Comics.
All Rights Reserved. All characters, their distinctive likenesses and related elements featured in this publication are trademarks of DC Comics.
The stories, characters and incidents featured in this publication are entirely fictional.
DC Comics does not read or accept unsolicited submissions of ideas, stories or artwork.

DC Comics, 2900 West Alameda Ave., Burbank, CA 91505
Printed by LSC Communications, Kendallville, IN, USA. 7/28/17. First Printing.
ISBN: 978-1-4012-7149-7

Library of Congress Cataloging-in-Publication Data is available.

PEACE IN OUR TIME

DAN ABNETT WRITER BRAD WALKER PENCILLER ANDREW HENNESSY INKER GABE ELTAEB COLORIST PAT BROSSEAU LETTERER
BRAD WALKER, ANDREW HENNESSY & GABE ELTAEB COVER
AMEDEO TURTURRO & DIEGO LOPEZ ASSISTANT EDITORS BRIAN CUNNINGHAM EDITOR

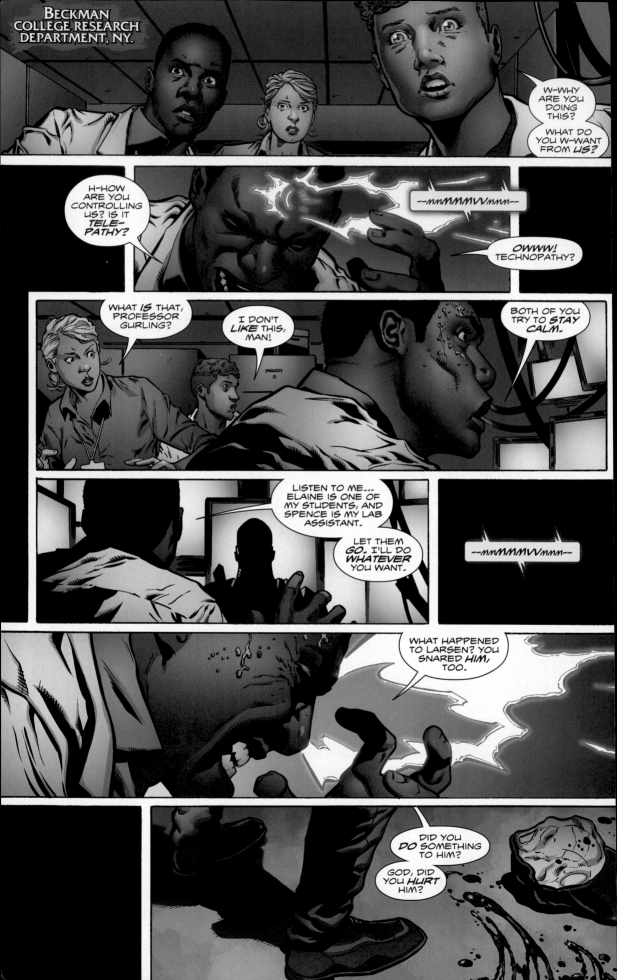

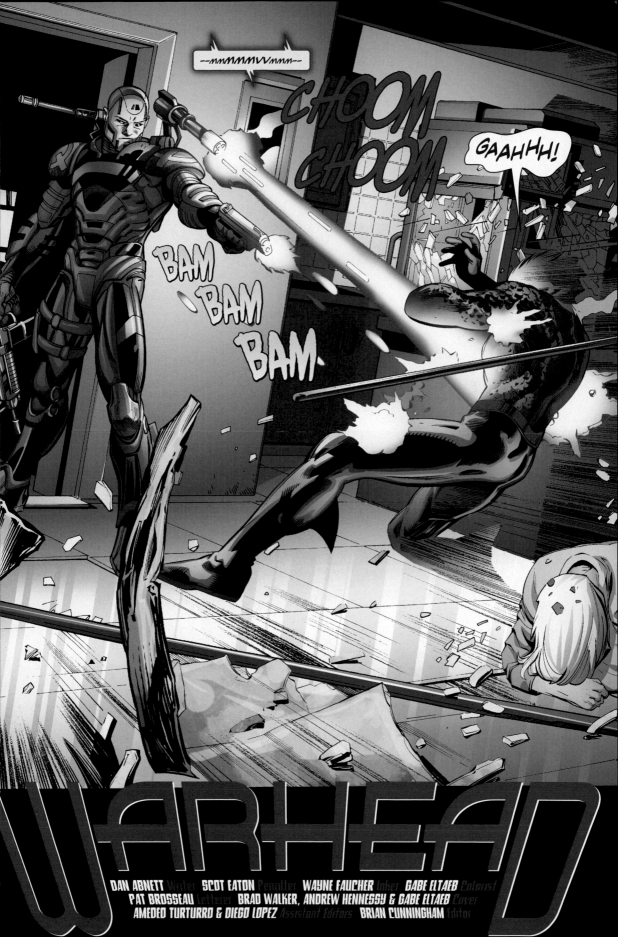

--mmMMMVmmm--

CHOOM CHOOM

GAAHHH!

BAM BAM BAM

WARHEAD

DAN ABNETT *Writer*   SCOT EATON *Penciller*   WAYNE FAUCHER *Inker*   GABE ELTAEB *Colorist*
PAT BROSSEAU *Letterer*   BRAD WALKER, ANDREW HENNESSY & GABE ELTAEB *Cover*
AMEDEO TURTURRO & DIEGO LOPEZ *Assistant Editors*   BRIAN CUNNINGHAM *Editor*

WE LOVE YOU, AQUAMAN!

YOU CAN SAVE ME ANYTIME!

ATLANTIS RULES!

THAT WHICH SANK MUST RISE AGAIN!

...AND A LEGION OF "AQUAFANS" GATHERING OUTSIDE THE UNITED NATIONS BUILDING IN NEW YORK TO CATCH A GLIMPSE OF THEIR HERO...

...THE KING OF ATLANTIS, WHO HAS RECEIVED GLOBAL PRAISE FOR HIS EFFORTS TO STOP THE RECENT WAR BETWEEN HIS KINGDOM AND THE SURFACE WORLD.

AMNESTY BAY, MASSACHUSETTS.

AT THE INVITATION OF THE WHITE HOUSE, AQUAMAN WILL BE ADDRESSING THE UNITED NATIONS GENERAL ASSEMBLY. THE FIRST TIME ATLANTIS HAS RECEIVED SUCH RECOGNITION FROM THE U.N.

MANY BELIEVE THAT ATLANTIS WILL BECOME A MEMBER OF THE U.N. BEFORE THE MIDDLE OF NEXT YEAR—

THIS IS SO EXCITING, RIGHT?

BECKMAN COLLEGE, NY.

SECRET SERVICE! DON'T MOVE!

AQUAMAN! WHERE IS HE?

H-HE'S IN THERE. IN THE LAB.

WITH WARHEAD.

WHAT WARHEAD?

NNHH! DOOR WON'T BUDGE!

ARTHUR CURRY! AQUAMAN!

THIS IS THE SECRET SERVICE!

OPEN THIS DOOR NOW!

SUPERPOWER

DAN ABNETT Writer   SCOT EATON Penciller   WAYNE FAUCHER Inker
GABE ELTAEB Colorist   PAT BROSSEAU Letterer   BRAD WALKER, ANDREW HENNESSY & GABE ELTAEB Cover
AMEDEO TURTURRO & DIEGO LOPEZ Assistant Editors   BRIAN CUNNINGHAM Editor

THIS IS THE WAR ZONE IN KAHNDAQ. IT FEELS REAL. *TOO* REAL.

BUT IT'S *NOT*.

NEPTUNE--!

PLEASE! *PLEASE!* IN THE NAME OF ALL THAT'S HOLY!

STOP THIS ATTACK! YOU ARE BOMBING *VILLAGES!* *FAMILIES!*

STOP THIS! *PLEASE!*

BIALYA HAS *SURRENDERED!* WE ARE NO LONGER *FIGHTING* YOU!

WE ARE *NOT* YOUR ENEMY! WE ARE N--

UHNN!

"...WE'RE HERE TO DISCOVER WHAT *CREATED* IT."

WELL, I'M ONLY HERE *BECAUSE* IT'S DEAD. PLUS, THE FEDS SAY MY COOPERATION WILL *GREASE THE WHEELS* AT TRIAL.

WHICH *ONE*, MORTIMER? PIRACY? ENDANGERMENT? THEFT OF ATLANTEAN ARTIFACTS—

HEH. CAN YOU EVEN *SEE* ME FROM UP ON THAT HIGH HORSE?

HEARD YOU WENT TO *WAR* WITH THE U.S. OF A.

SIR, THE BRIEF SAID IT WAS MORTIMER HERE WHO FIRST ENCOUNTERED THE... "STRANGE WATER" STUFF.

DURING AN ILLEGAL SALVAGE OPERATION. HE DIDN'T REPORT IT TO THE AUTHORITIES.

ONE OF HIS CREW, A MAN CALLED JONAH PAYNE, CAME IN CONTACT WITH THE SUBSTANCE. LATER, PAYNE BECAME A MONSTER.

I'M *SURE* YOU CAN EMPATHIZE.

THE PRESS DUBBED THE CREATURE *DEAD WATER.* THE FINAL BODY COUNT WAS *THIRTEEN.*

AGENTS IRVING AND AJAR BROUGHT ME IN TO CONSULT ON THE CASE, AND WE EVENTUALLY *STOPPED* THE RAMPAGE.

PAYNE *DIDN'T* SURVIVE. I...I WANT TO KNOW WHAT *DID* THAT TO HIM.

AGREED. LET'S HAUL.

WEAPONS HOT.

VZZZMMMM

COPY. HYPER-GUNS ARMED.

VZZZMMMM

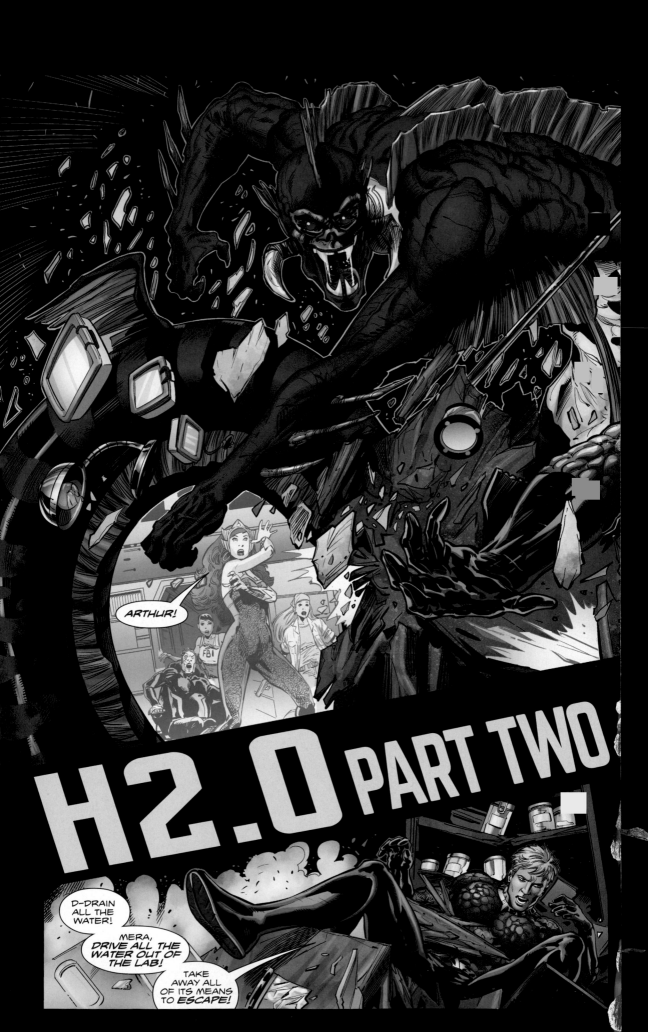

DAN ABNETT WRITER PHILIPPE BRIONES ARTIST GABE ELTAEB COLORIST PAT BROSSEAU LETTERER
BRAD WALKER, ANDREW HENNESSY & GABE ELTAEB COVER AMEDEO TURTURRO & DIEGO LOPEZ ASSISTANT EDITORS BRIAN CUNNINGHAM EDITOR

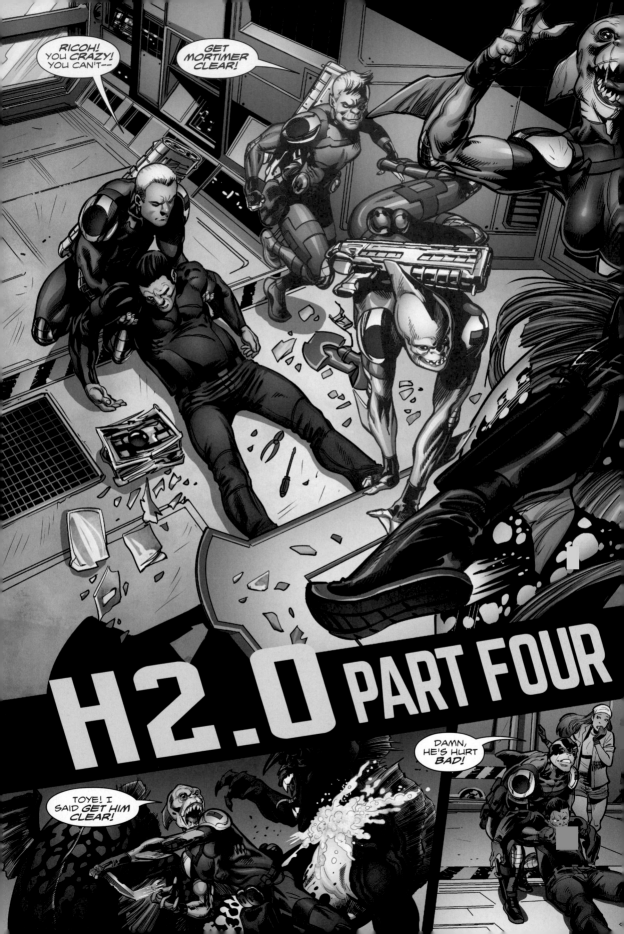

DAN ABNETT WRITER PHILIPPE BRIONES ARTIST GABE ELTAEB COLORIST PAT BROSSEAU LETTERER
BRAD WALKER, ANDREW HENNESSY & GABE ELTAEB COVER BRIAN CUNNINGHAM GROUP EDITOR
HARVEY RICHARDS ASSOCIATE EDITOR ANDY KHOURI EDITOR

WHAT? NO!

OH GOD, IT'S BACK...

HELP ME, REAGAN!

WHERE'S ARNI? ARNI WAS IN HERE!

I— IT IS... ARNI...

NIGHTFALL.

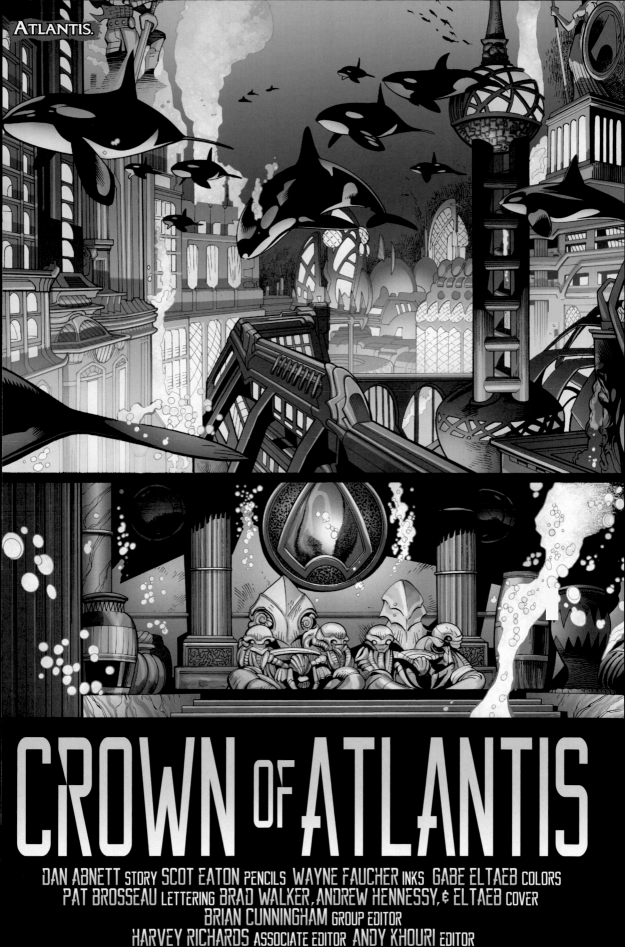

ATLANTIS.

CROWN OF ATLANTIS

DAN ABNETT STORY SCOT EATON PENCILS WAYNE FAUCHER INKS GABE ELTAEB COLORS
PAT BROSSEAU LETTERING BRAD WALKER, ANDREW HENNESSY, & ELTAEB COVER
BRIAN CUNNINGHAM GROUP EDITOR
HARVEY RICHARDS ASSOCIATE EDITOR ANDY KHOURI EDITOR

HE IS SAYING, MERA OF XEBEL, THAT HE AND HIS WARRIORS WERE RELEASED BY *OUR* AUTHORITY.

THE PENITENTIARY VAULT, ATLANTIS.

CROWN OF THORNS

DAN ABNETT story SCOT EATON & PHILIPPE BRIONES pencils
WAYNE FAUCHER PHILIPPE BRIONES & SCOTT HANNA inks GABE ELTAEB colors
PAT BROSSEAU lettering BRAD WALKER, ANDREW HENNESSY, & GABE ELTAEB cover
BRIAN CUNNINGHAM group editor HARVEY RICHARDS associate editor
ANDY KHOURI editor AQUAMAN created by PAUL NORRIS

SO ONCE HE HAS *DONE* HIS DUTY, AND SAID ALL HE CAN TO CHANGE THEIR MINDS, HE WILL SEE WHAT I HAVE *ALREADY* SEEN...

...THE *FUTILITY* OF ARGUING WITH A NATION THAT IS TOO *SCARED* TO LISTEN TO REASON.

HE'LL COME TO ME, WITH HIS HEART *BROKEN.*

AND I WILL HELP HIM *HEAL.*

WILL YOU... LIVE *HERE,* IN AMNESTY BAY?

I WILL BECOME HIS *WIFE,* FOR THERE WILL BE NO *ROYAL BURDEN* TO KEEP US APART ANYMORE.

TULA, I NEVER WANTED TO MARRY A *KING* OR BE A *QUEEN.* I JUST WANTED TO LOVE *ARTHUR CU--*

MERA! THERE!

BOOOM

WHAT IN NEPTUNE'S NAME IS THAT?

TULA--

--STAY HERE.

AQUAMAN #16 variant cover by JOSHUA MIDDLETON

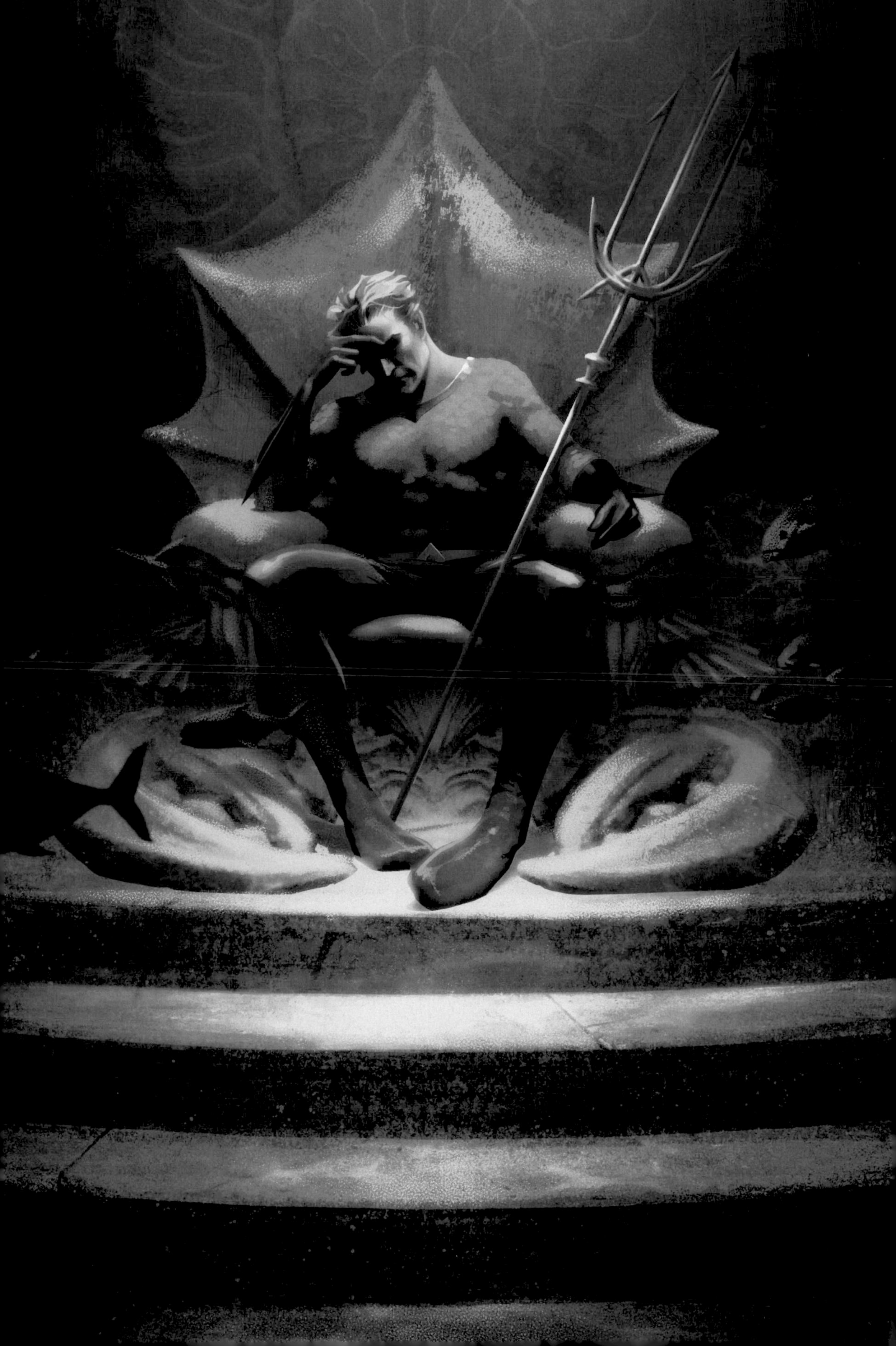

AQUAMAN #17 variant cover by JOSHUA MIDDLETON

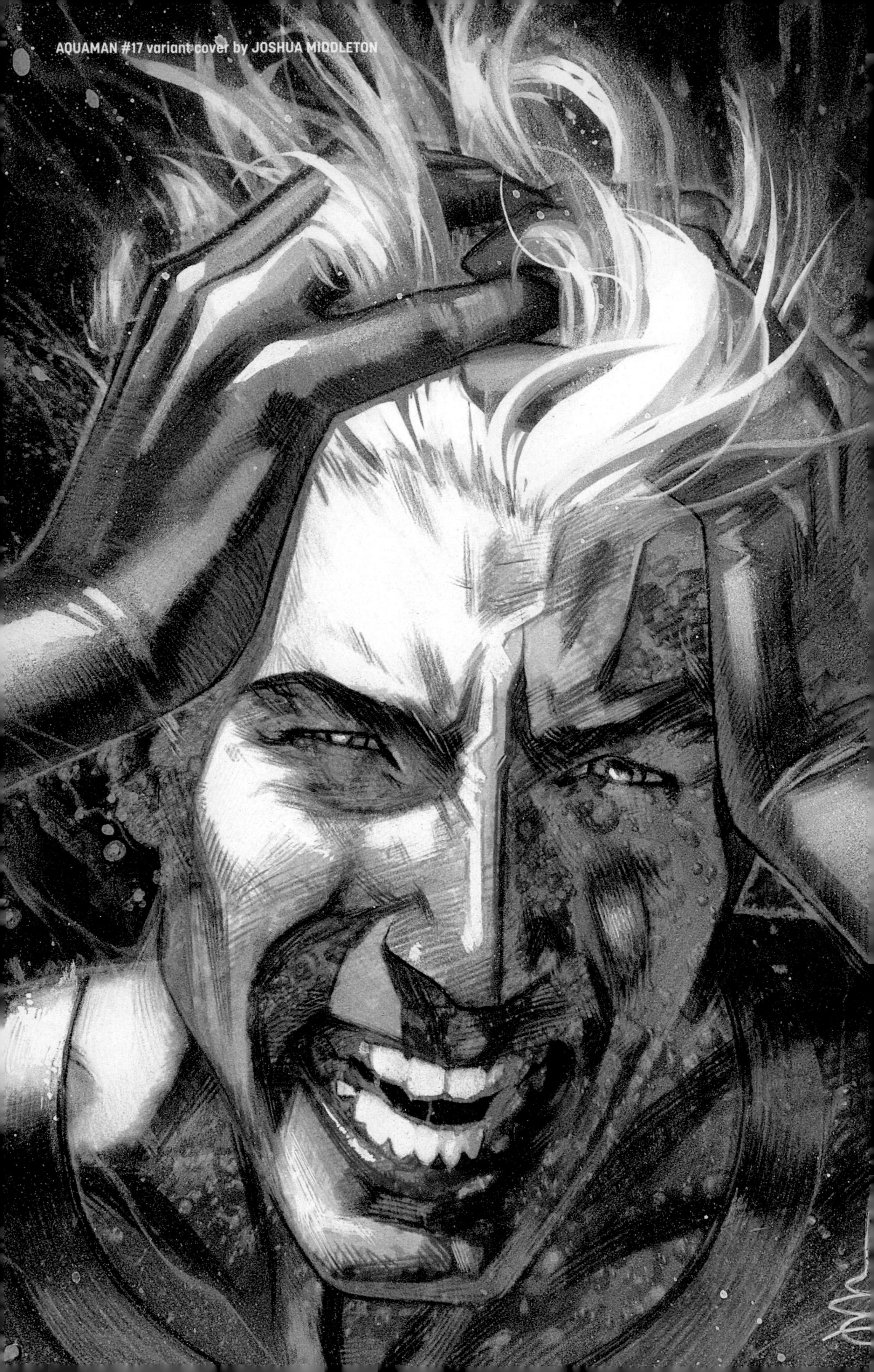

AQUAMAN #18 variant cover by JOSHUA MIDDLETON

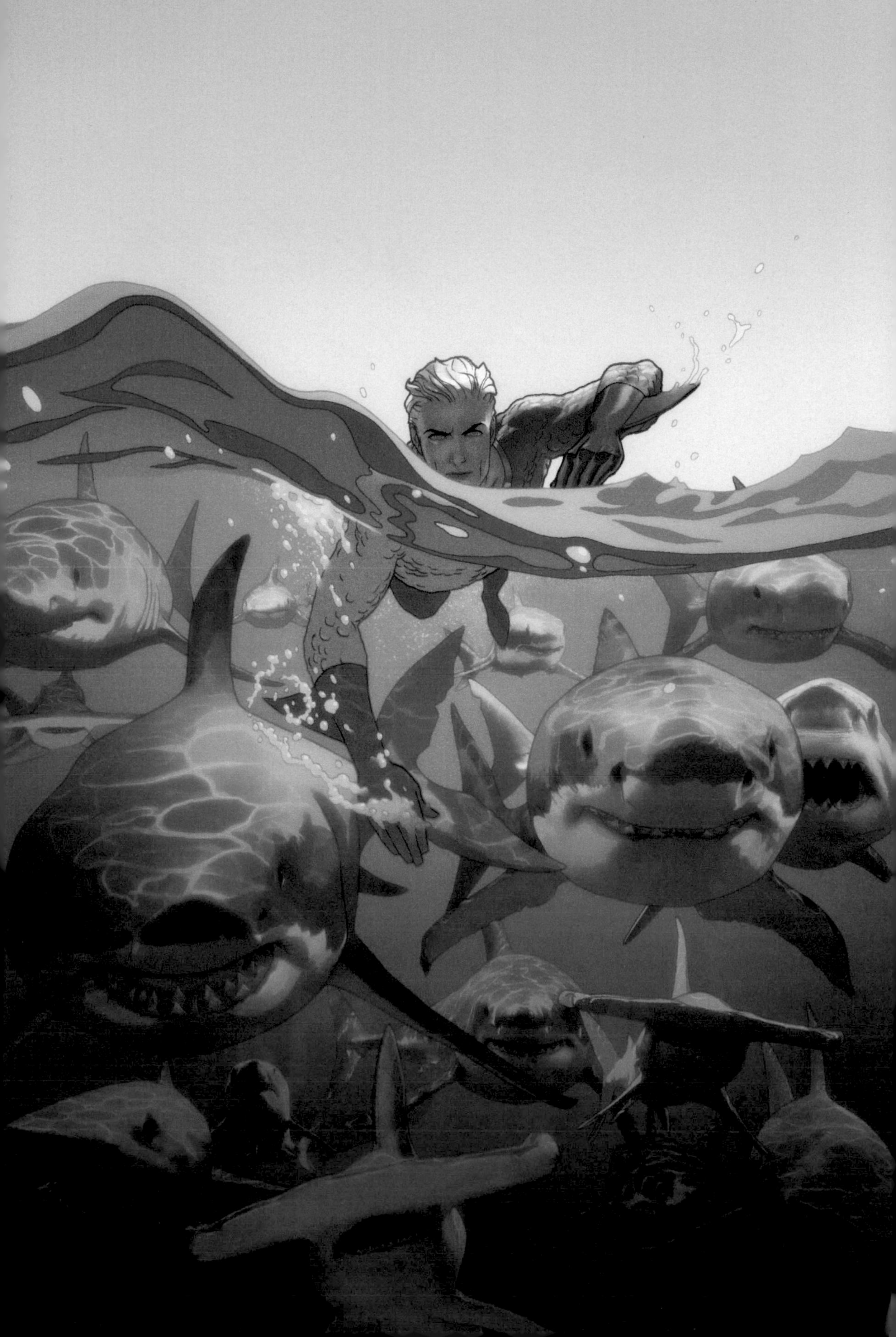

AQUAMAN #20 variant cover by JOSHUA MIDDLETON

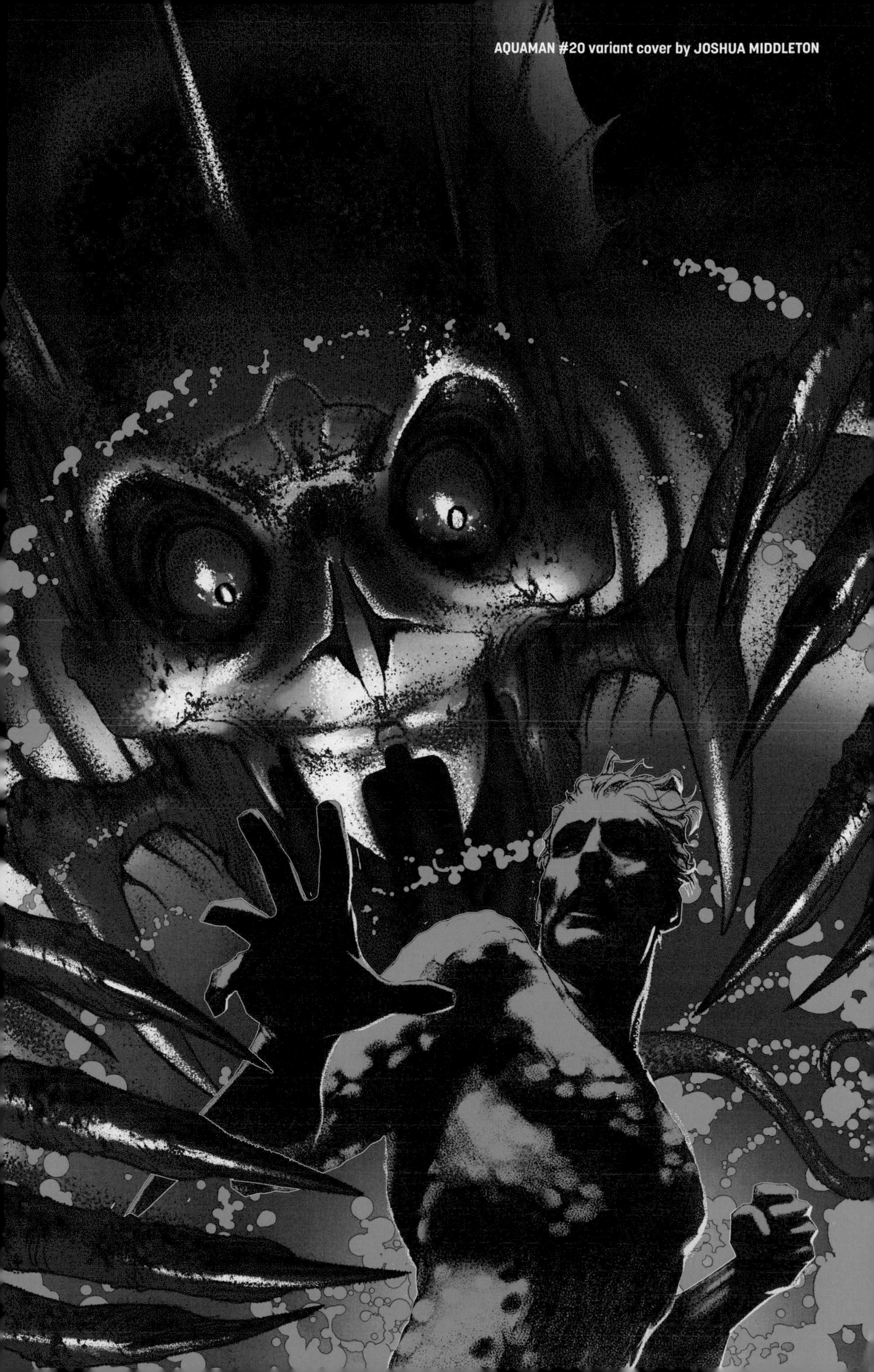

AQUAMAN #21 variant cover by JOSHUA MIDDLETON

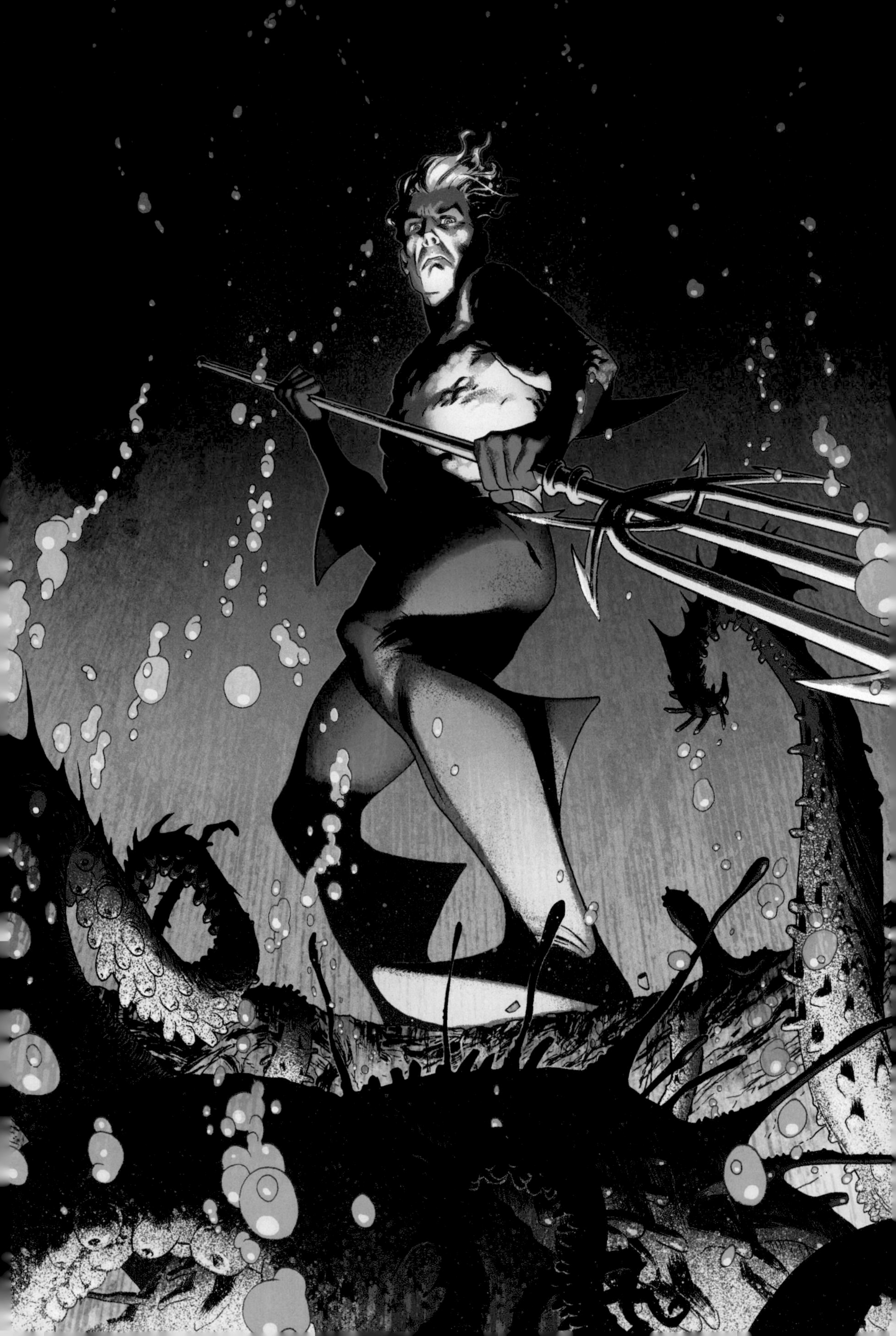

AQUAMAN #22 variant cover by JOSHUA MIDDLETON

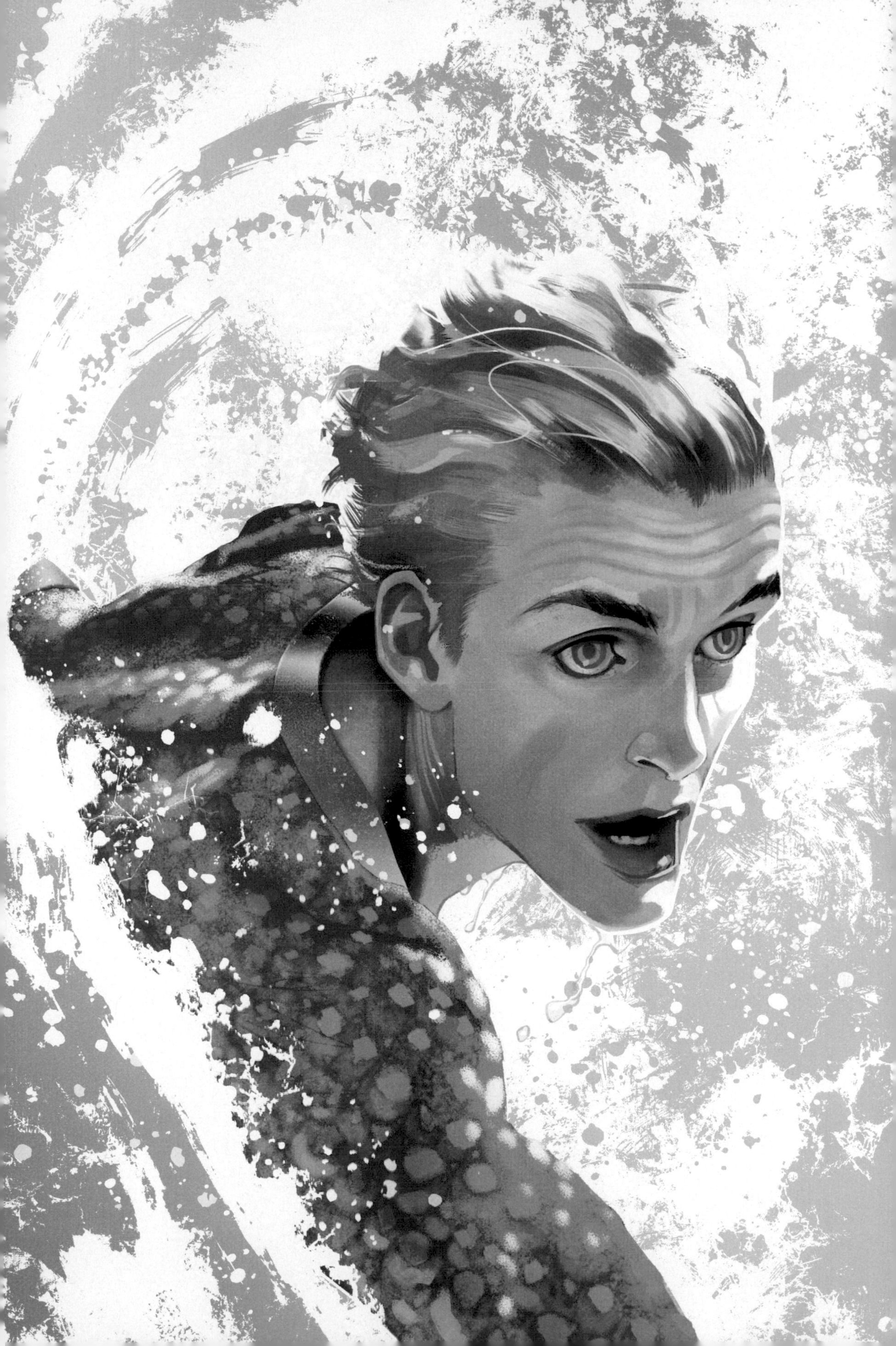

AQUAMAN #23 variant cover by JOSHUA MIDDLETON

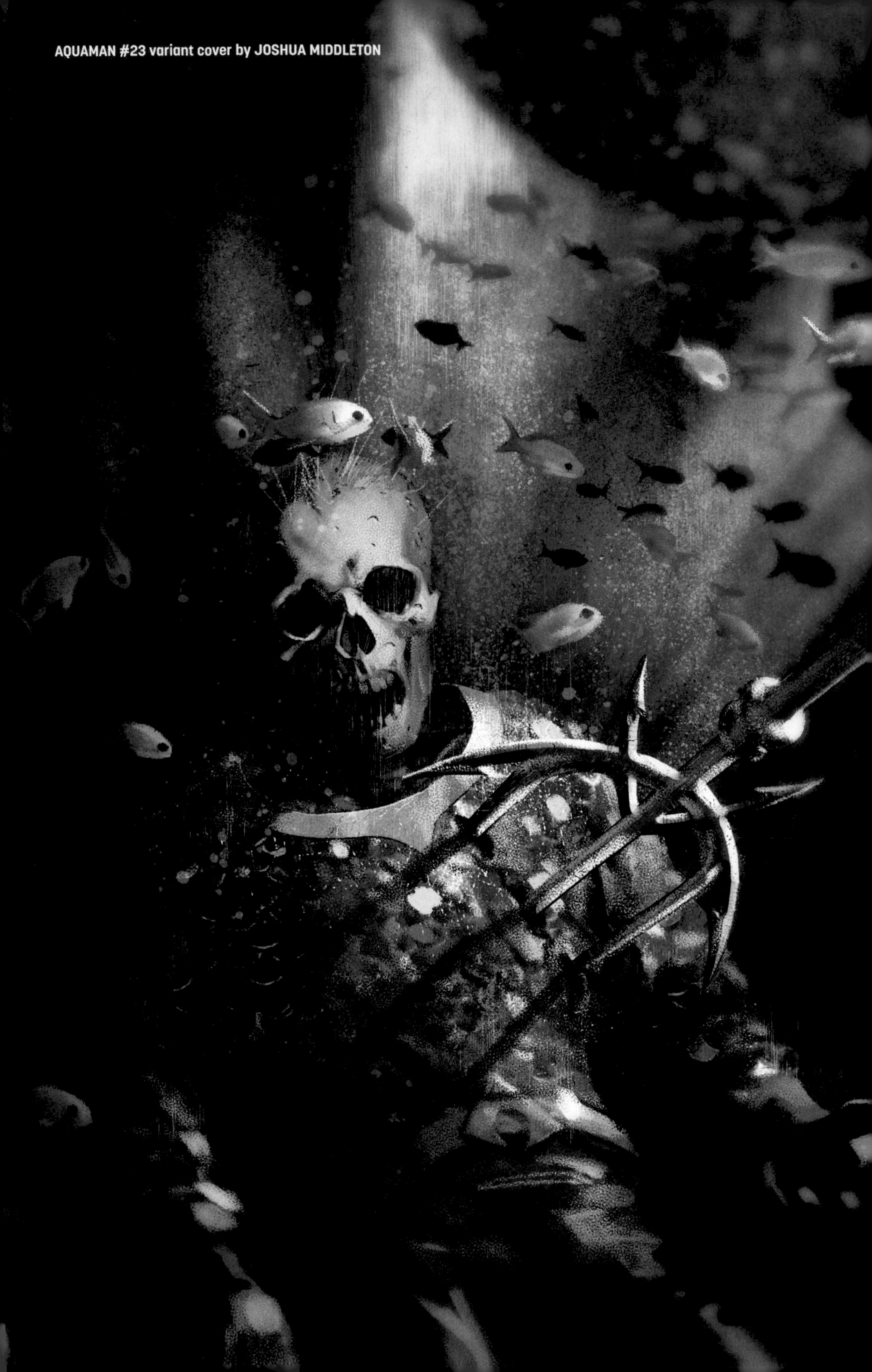

AQUAMAN #24 variant cover by JOSHUA MIDDLETON

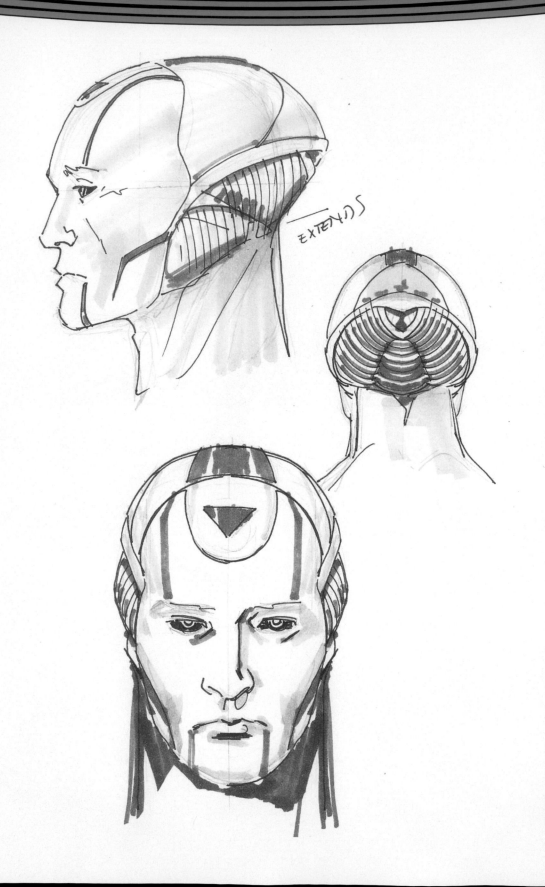

EXTENDS

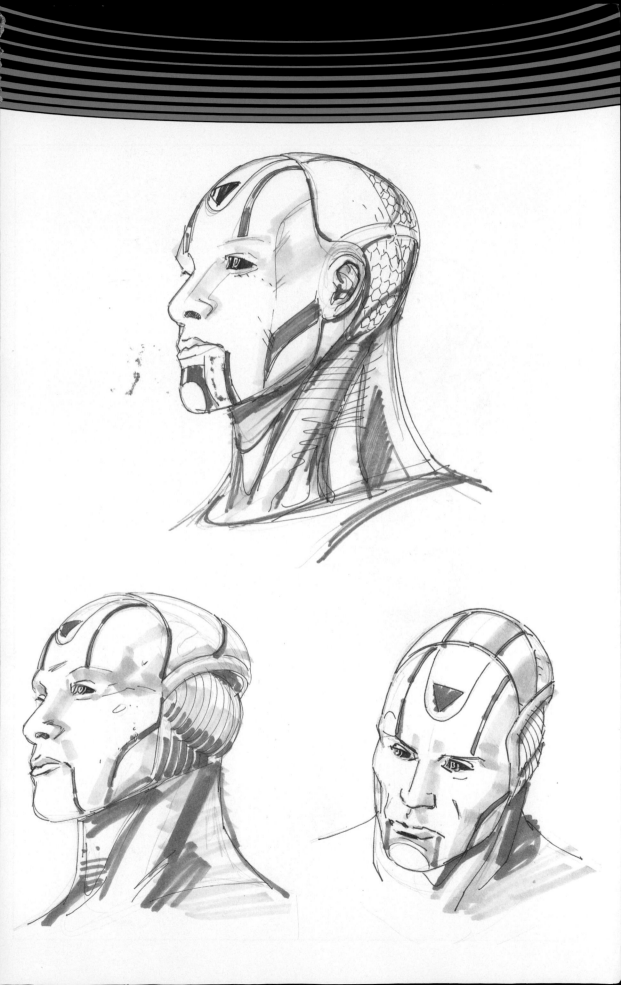

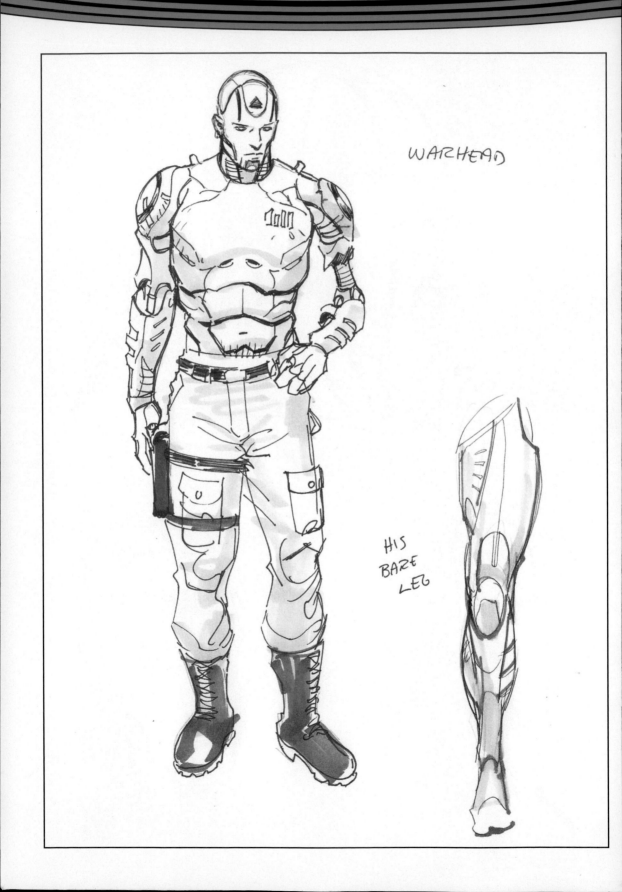

WARHEAD

HIS
BARE
LEG

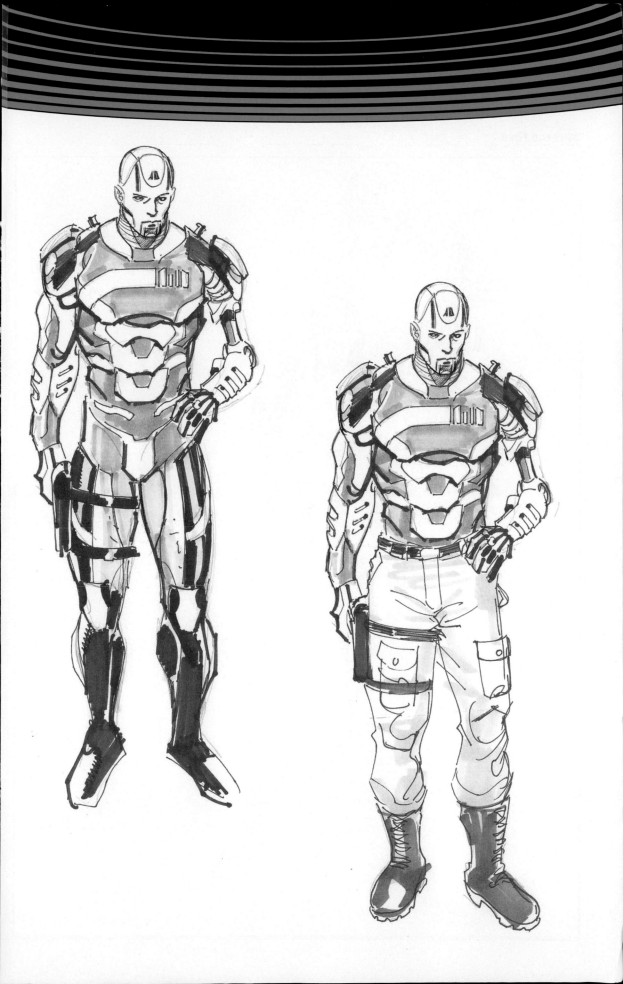

Warhead Final